THE
KITCHEN
without
BORDERS

RECIPES AND STORIES FROM REFUGEE AND IMMIGRANT CHEFS

THE EAT OFFBEAT CHEFS

PHOTOGRAPHY BY
PENNY DE LOS SANTOS

WORKMAN PUBLISHING ✳ NEW YORK

Library of Congress Cataloging-in-Publication Data is available.
ISBN 978-1-5235-0404-6

Written and recipes tested by Siobhan Wallace
Original photography by Penny De Los Santos
Chef Juan Suarez de Lezo photography by Bea Merry
Food stylist: Nora Singley
Prop stylist: Sara Abalan

Back cover credit: Olga Vasilyeva/Shutterstock.com (Linen Texture)
Additional credit: StockAppeal/Shutterstock.com (Globe Icon)

Workman books are available at special discounts when purchased in
bulk for premiums and sales promotions as well as for fund-raising or
educational use. Special editions or book excerpts can also be created
to specification. For details, contact the Special Sales Director at the
address below, or send an email to specialmarkets@workman.com.

Workman Publishing Company, Inc.
225 Varick Street
New York, NY 10014-4381
workman.com

Workman is a registered trademark of Workman Publishing Co., Inc.

Printed in South Korea
First printing May 2020

10 9 8 7 6 5 4 3 2 1

FOR ALL THE TALENTED AND
HARD-WORKING REFUGEES AND IMMIGRANTS
AROUND THE WORLD, AND THE WELCOMING
COMMUNITIES WHO HELP THEM BLOSSOM
TO CREATE A BETTER FUTURE TOGETHER.

AND FOR THE EAT OFFBEAT CHEFS,
WHOSE AMAZING TALENT,
PASSION, AND DEDICATION MADE
THIS ADVENTURE POSSIBLE.

CONTENTS

OUR STORY

A note from Wissam and Manal,
co-founders of Eat Offbeat

THE INHERITANCE OF FLAVOR

This story starts like so many other cooking stories—with a grandmother's recipe.

When Manal moved to New York City in 2013, she was very disappointed with the quality of the supermarket hummus—it did not even come close to the amazing taste and texture of our grandmother's recipe back home in Lebanon. Hummus is ubiquitous throughout the Middle East, with a variety of interpretations and many countries claiming ownership of the "authentic" original recipe. We won't attempt to resolve that quarrel, but this particular version came with our grandmother from her hometown in Aleppo, Syria, so it is authentic to us. It was the hummus we grew up with.

Manal, craving a taste of home, began to make batches of our Syrian grandmother's hummus regularly, and word got out among our friends in New York. They raved about it so much that we asked ourselves, "Why not share this hummus with everyone?"

What we quickly realized was that the success had only a little to do with the hummus itself and much more to do with the story behind it. It carried memories from a faraway and mysterious land. Our audience had heard of Syria in the news, but under much different circumstances—they were familiar with a country ravaged by fighting, not with stories of a rich, generational food culture. Our grandmother's hummus had a certain mystique—it was the same one that families in Aleppo shared around their kitchen tables centuries ago, and still enjoy today, on sunny terraces in the shadows of grapevines. This recipe conveyed memories of happiness, a far cry from the wars and violence that our guests heard about on the news.

And so it has been for the many other of countries that people fled, looking for a better life, often leaving everything behind except for their beautiful memories immortalized in the recipes they brought along with them. These tasty dishes represent cultures in which cooking is valued as an act of love for family, not just an elevated art that professionals practice in restaurants.

With this seed of an idea, Eat Offbeat—a catering company that hires talented refugees who have come to call New York City home and serves their dishes to businesses and individuals across the city—began.

THE FIRST STEP OFF THE EATEN PATH

Our company, Eat Offbeat, was born out of the desire to give life to the special food memories our chefs brought with them. In our kitchen, they can share their stories through the most intimate form of expression—cooking their own dishes the way they would cook them for their families. This was a language New Yorkers understood instantly. Those who came once to support Eat Offbeat's mission came back and brought their friends because they loved the food and what it conveyed.

In a city that seemingly has every type of regional food you could think of, these amazing chefs uncovered something truly new: They not only introduced New Yorkers to different cuisines (Nepali, Iraqi, Syrian, Sri Lankan, Eritrean, and so on), but they built a bridge to connect to the community and share their talents. It was a reinvention of the catering experience: From a purely functional purpose, it became something truly experiential that challenged preconceived notions and stigmas. In an era where everything is about "authentic" experiences, the Eat Offbeat chefs took authenticity to the next level.

THE SOUL BEHIND THE FOOD

As we remember dishes that are significant to us, it's not perfection, but imperfection,

that makes them special and memorable. It's the hint of extra garlic that reminds us of our grandmother's unique touch or the extra sauce that makes us recognize, without any doubt, our mother's recipe. What's more, these personal tweaks are the ultimate expression of a caring chef.

When asked by a TV reporter about what cooking meant to her, Chef Nasrin, whom you'll meet on page 24, answered: "Food is love." One could have mistakenly attributed this simple answer to her limited English vocabulary back then, but the passion sparkling in her eyes and the sincerity in her voice made it more eloquent than an answer any Michelin-starred chef could have given.

You see, if you observe the Eat Offbeat chefs in our Long Island City kitchen, you will notice an unparalleled passion for and dedication to their craft. This is because they don't perceive their work as just preparing food—they yearn to create a special bond with New Yorkers. The chefs see this as an opportunity to bring something unique from their cultures to our guests. They take immense pride in sharing their cuisines, and put in love, as if they were cooking for their own families. Emotions—pride, dignity, love, and the desire to connect—can't be faked, and once again authenticity is redefined.

BE OUR GUESTS AT THIS TABLE

There is a famous Middle Eastern saying: *Sar fi beynatna khobz wa meleh,* meaning "Now there is bread and salt between us." This idiom is used to illustrate how eating together will cement the relationship between two people. We once heard a very wise refugee give his own interpretation of the saying: "Nobody can hate me after they have tasted my mother's hummus."

We hope that as you read our story and sit down to share this food with others, you will allow the story of our common human experience to serve as a platform for deeper connection. We also hope this book will help you learn about our team, especially our chefs, and maybe give you a different perspective on who we all are and where we all come from.

Most importantly, as you prepare these delicious recipes, don't forget to mix in your own version of love, passion, and pride—three truly essential ingredients for the success of every dish!

MANAL AND WISSAM KAHI

LEBANON

MANAL AND WISSAM KAHI (PICTURED, PAGE XII) DIDN'T SET OUT TO START a catering company. They originally wanted to sell hummus inspired by their Syrian grandmother's recipe (page 23), and felt this could possibly be a good way to help recent Syrian refugees ground themselves in a new country.

As the idea for the company came together, the siblings, who grew up in a very socially conscious environment, wanted to add a social element. Since their home-land, Lebanon, is a major destination for Syrian refugees, helping the displaced Syrians who are sent to New York made sense. But as the idea expanded to include more than just hummus, it began to include more than just Syrian refugees as well. Slowly, Eat Offbeat formed.

Manal and Wissam grew up surrounded by good food. Their family comes from Sehayleh, Lebanon, a village about a half hour northeast of Beirut. Manal and Wissam, along with their sister, Hala, and their parents, lived in a homestead filled with extended family, surrounding an orchard. Both parents worked, which was unusual for the time. And while she does cook quite well, their mother was able to leave a lot of the daily cooking to her mother and an aunt. "They were both amazing cooks; everything was top-notch," says Manal. "We can't cook as well as they can!"

The orchard not only provided most of the produce the families needed, it also gave the children a place to play. Manal fondly remembers the smell of blooming orange and mandarin trees, but it's the *janerik* (sour green plums) that she misses the most. "We'd climb the tree and our grandmother would come yell at us to not eat them all," she says. The pull of the janerik is so strong, Manal now times her trips back to coincide with the month-long harvest season.

For Wissam, it's the green almonds. "I would climb the tree and just eat them for hours," he says. Though separated by eleven years, the two are close enough that when Manal was ready to leave Lebanon for the States, having Wissam in New York City was comforting. He had just put down roots in New York City in the early 2010s when Manal was accepted to Columbia's School of International and Public Affairs (SIPA).

Manal's move to New York wasn't as jarring as her earlier sojourns to Spain and Germany, but as time went on, she found she missed the food from home. That's

how the calls back home for recipes started. "It would make their day when we'd call asking how to make something," says Manal. And then there was the hummus.

As the idea for a company involving refugees formed, Manal and Wissam looked for feedback from outside sources. Their first validation was winning the Tamer Fund for Social Ventures in 2015. Every semester, the Tamer Center for Social Enterprise, a part of the Columbia Business School, runs the competition for Columbia University's students, alumni, and faculty, with the best business plans awarded seed grants of up to $25,000. The competition not only encourages participants to form businesses with social justice aspects but also teaches the business school students to analyze the plans. Of those submissions, Manal and Wissam's plan was one of the five awardees. Knowing that others thought they were on the right track helped Manal and Wissam gain confidence. "If we hadn't won, there wouldn't have been a business," Manal says. "It helped us not only financially but psychologically."

Another validation came from the International Rescue Committee (IRC). One of the IRC's missions is to help refugees rebuild their lives. Having them on board was crucial to Eat Offbeat's formation. Not only could they connect Manal and Wissam with refugees who wanted to cook, they could help with feedback.

The first meal prepared at the Eat Offbeat kitchen was cooked in November 2015. The siblings collaborated with four people: three cooks plus Chef Juan Suarez de Lezo, a seasoned chef with experience in various Michelin-starred restaurants who became Eat Offbeat's chief culinary officer (see page 200). Those first menus included Rachana's Vegetable Momos (page 2), Mitslal's Adas (page 112), and Dhuha's Sumac Salad (page 44).

Over time, the Eat Offbeat kitchen expanded its staff and its menu. The first crew included immigrants from five countries: Iraq, Nepal, Eritrea, Spain, and Lebanon. Within three years, that number expanded to chefs from fifteen countries. The menu has included more than sixty items over the same time period, with about twenty-five dishes available at any given time.

As one factor in their success, Manal points to a trait all the Eat Offbeat employees have learned through their life journeys: the ability to adapt. When people are immigrating or are displaced from their homes, they must adapt to ever-changing circumstances. That skill helps them in the kitchen when the unexpected happens. And it will continue to help the entire Eat Offbeat family as they continue to grow the company and change lives.

THE EAT OFFBEAT PANTRY

Ingredients, Sourcing, and Substitutions

Although many of these dishes rely on simple techniques and are accessible versions of familiar foods, some ingredients that might be less familiar to a Western audience are included—heightening the flavor profile and adding a special quality to the dishes without a lot of extra fuss. If a reasonable substitution is available, it will be listed here. Sometimes an ingredient is too unique to be replaced, such as asafetida powder, so in those instances, omitting the ingredient is an option, although keep in mind that the dish won't quite maintain the intended flavor.

ACHIOTINA

Classic Latin American dishes like *cochinita pibil* (shredded pork), *longaniza* (spicy pork sausage similar to chorizo), and *hallacas* (tamales—page 164) get their yellowish-red color from *achiotina* or achiote paste. Achiote paste is made by grinding annatto seeds with garlic and savory spices. The paste can then be infused into lard or dissolved in acidic liquids like lemon juice and vinegar. Jars of the lard-based achiotina can be found with Latin American ingredients in most major supermarkets, and blocks of achiote paste can be found in specialty stores.

ASAFETIDA POWDER

Also known as *hing* powder, asafetida comes from the resin of giant fennel plants (part of the celery family) found in Afghanistan, Iran, and India. Asafetida is closely identified with South Asian cuisine, where it is found in lentil curries and *rogan josh* (a red lamb stew), but it is also used in Ayurvedic medicine and as a digestive aid. While the resin is sold in chunks overseas, Westerners will usually find it ground and bottled, often with a neutral additive like wheat flour. The spice's sulfur aromas mellow out while cooking, resulting in a balanced umami flavor similar to that of leeks. Due to its pungency, asafetida should be added to dishes in very small amounts, and it should be stored in an airtight container.

BERBERE SPICES

Named after the Amharic word for "pepper" or "hot," this spice blend comes from Ethiopian and Eritrean cuisine. Although the ratio and ingredients can vary, the savory elements of most blends will come from allspice, black peppercorns, carom seeds, cinnamon, coriander, fenugreek seeds, ginger, green cardamom, nigella seeds, nutmeg, onion flakes, paprika, or *korarima*, a wild cardamom native to Ethiopia. The heat so typical of berbere spices typically derives from chiles de árbol.

Preground mixes are widely available in some large grocers or at specialty spice stores and online, but toasting and grinding your own spices is always preferred.

BIRD'S-EYE CHILE

Also known as the Thai chile and piri piri, this thin little green or red chile pepper is commonly used in dishes from southeast Asia to eastern Africa. The peppers are closer in heat to habaneros than jalapeños, but either can be used as a substitute.

CAMEROON BLACK PEPPER

Also known as *Nsukka* pepper and Ghana pepper, this aromatic, very hot, reddish-brown spice is made from dried Scotch bonnet peppers and is found in Nigerian dishes. It can often be found in markets dedicated to African ingredients, but habaneros, Kashmiri chiles, or cayenne pepper can be used as a substitute.

CHAR MAGAZ

Whether used in traditional desserts or ground into a paste to thicken dishes, the traditional blend for *char magaz* is composed of dried seeds from pumpkins, cantaloupes, watermelons, and cucumbers. Char magaz is frequently used in Rajasthani and other northern Indian dishes.

CURRY LEAVES

These aromatic, shiny green leaves from the curry leaf plant—not the curry plant nor related to curry powder—are essential to South Asian cuisine. The herb has a citrus-y smell and imparts a little bitterness and heat to dishes to round out the other flavors.

Packets of fresh leaves are easy to find refrigerated at specialty grocers and online, and any extra leaves can be frozen for use within a year—just bruise the frozen leaf before adding it to a dish. Dried curry leaves are also available but are less pungent.

FENUGREEK

Common in curry dishes and tea blends from the western Mediterranean to the Indian subcontinent, this herb is even used in fake maple syrup. Finding it fresh is very rare—you're more likely to come across the seeds and the dried leaves, which will sometimes be called by their Indian name, *kasoori methi*. Both add a certain bittersweet quality to the final dish, and there's no real substitute.

JACKFRUIT

Native to southeast Asia, this tropical fruit appears often in Indian, Bangladeshi, Nepalese, and Thai recipes. You may also know of it from vegan recipes, where it's used to replace meat, as in "jackfruit pulled pork." The meat of jackfruit is starchy and stringy, with a flavor close to that of papaya when unripe. It does get sweeter as it ripens, leading to a tropical flavor like that of pineapple. You can find the fruit canned in brine at most major grocery stores, and whole jackfruits and freshly cut portions are often found in the produce section at Asian markets.

For whole unripe green fruits, wait until the skin turns yellowish, the flesh softens, and it emits a musky smell before cutting it open. The fruit has sticky sap. For easier cutting and cleanup, it helps to coat your kitchen knife with cooking spray. Cut the fruit lengthwise into quarters, core it, and detach the flesh from the fibrous filaments. The flesh is okay to eat raw, but the seeds need to be boiled and peeled before being consumed.

JIMBU

A cornerstone of Nepali cuisine, this allium tastes similar to other mild members of the onion family, like dried wild garlic and dried chives. In most specialty grocery stores, *jimbu* is sold as fine dried strands. To enhance its flavor, it can be lightly fried in oil or ghee before being added to dishes.

KASHK BIBI

Kashk bibi is a common ingredient from Iran to the Balkans. It's made from fermented yogurt, milk, or whey leftover from making cheese. Then it's mixed with wheat or barley, resulting in a distinct umami flavor similar to Parmesan. It's typically used to thicken and add flavor to sauces, soups, and stews. But it is a vital ingredient in a number of dips like Kashk Bademjan (page 30) and can be a wonderful addition to Baba Ghannoush (page 33). In addition to jarred liquid kashk, the condiment can be found in dehydrated spheres that keep for up to a year. Note that once a jar of kashk is open, it keeps in the fridge for only a week or two.

KASHMIRI CHILE

Looks are deceiving with this Indian chile. Its vibrant red color doesn't denote spice. Instead, it's rather mild with a heat level close to a poblano. Dried chiles can be found whole and then ground at home when needed, but Kashmiri chile powder is making its way into the mainstream grocery market, so look for it in the spice aisle.

MAGGI SAUCE

Popular throughout the world, Maggi sauces are versatile ingredients. Used most frequently in this book are the tomato-based Hot & Sweet Tomato Chilli Sauce and the Sweet Chili Sauce, both of which come from Maggi's South Asian product lines. However, the original dark seasoning sauce was created in the late 1800s by a Swiss inventor. It's important to note that many Maggi products have regional differences. For instance, the Mexican "jugo" version is more concentrated and saltier than the Chinese version.

PILONCILLO

Also known as *panela,* this Latin American ingredient made of unrefined whole cane sugar can be found in a variety of shapes, from cones to small disks that need to be grated to use. Piloncillo's deep, almost smoky flavor, sometimes with notes of caramel, will remind many of another sugar product: rum. You can substitute dark brown sugar for piloncillo, one for one. Jaggery, another cane sugar with date or palm sap, is also a good substitute.

POMEGRANATE MOLASSES

This Middle Eastern syrup isn't sugar-based molasses—it's pomegranate juice boiled down to an almost sour reduction. The final syrup is mildly sweet and tangy and is used in a variety of dishes, including Persian *Fesenjan* (page 136). Drizzle it in coffee for an elevated twist on your morning cup.

SEVEN SPICES

Also known as *sabaa baharat*, this blend of spices is found throughout the Middle East and Greece. Though the spices and herbs used vary from cuisine to cuisine and household to household, the aromatic mix usually includes allspice, cinnamon, cardamom, nutmeg, and cloves. You'll often find it labeled as Lebanese seven spices or Moroccan seven spices.

SHAWARMA SPICES

Part of the deliciousness of Middle Eastern shawarma comes from the spices that are used to flavor the meat before cooking. The usual combination includes allspice, asafetida, black pepper, cardamom, cayenne, cinnamon, coriander, cumin, garlic, paprika, sumac, and turmeric.

SUMAC

Purple, citrus-y, and tart sumac powder is made from the dried fruit of sumac flowers. Ground sumac can be used to brighten and complement a number of dishes, from a dusting on fresh bread and hummus to a garnish on brownies.

WRAPPERS

A few of the recipes in this book call for wrappers of some sort. For dumpling wrappers, look for the thin round wrappers, usually found in the freezer section—make sure to keep frozen until you're ready to use them. They are very susceptible to drying out, so keep them under a damp towel as you fill and seal them. For the thicker wrappers, look for frozen empanada wrappers, sometimes labeled as disks.

ZERESHK

Barberries, known as *zereshk* in Persian, are found in numerous dishes from Iran. Though the resilient plants can grow throughout the world, including in North America, the eastern Iranian province of South Khorasan is the largest producer of barberries. Because most of the commercial crops are grown in Iran, it's rare to find fresh barberries outside of the Middle East. Instead, you'll find these small, tangy red fruits in dried form at international markets and Middle Eastern grocers. In a pinch, unsweetened dried cranberries or currants can be substituted.

WHERE TO BUY

Most of the ingredients in this book are becoming more widely available, popping up in grocery stores as tastes change and palates broaden. For any ingredients that can't be found in your local grocery store or at international supermarkets, look online at Kalustyan's (foodsofnations.com), Patel Brothers (patelbros.com), Snuk Foods (snukfoods.com), and Tropical Appétit (tropicalappetit.com).

APPETIZERS AND DIPS

VEGETABLE MOMOS

*Steamed dumplings stuffed
with spiced, shredded cabbage;
spinach and paneer cheese;
or carrots and ginger*

— 2 —

BEEF KIBBEH

*Hand-shaped beef-and-bulgur
croquettes with seven spices*

— 7 —

POTATO KIBBEH

*Hand-shaped potato croquettes
stuffed with beef and herbs*

— 11 —

FATAYER

*Hand pies stuffed with
chicken, peppers, pomegranate
molasses, and Cheddar*

— 13 —

SAMOSAS

*Fried hand pies
with spiced potato filling*

— 16 —

CACHAPAS

*Corn cakes topped
with melted butter and cheese*

— 19 —

KUKU SABZI

Persian herbed frittata

— 20 —

HUMMUS

Chickpea dip with tahini and lemon

— 23 —

MIRZA GHASEMI

*Charred eggplant dip with
stewed tomatoes, onion, and garlic*

— 28 —

KASHK BADEMJAN

Turmeric-spiced eggplant and onion dip

— 30 —

BABA GHANNOUSH

Roasted eggplant dip with tahini

— 33 —

BORANI ESFENAJ

Creamy spinach dip

— 36 —

MUSABBAHA

Tahini-dressed chickpea salad

— 39 —

ZEYTOON PARVARDEH

Olive, pomegranate, and walnut tapenade

— 40 —

— VEGETABLE MOMOS —

Steamed dumplings stuffed with spiced, shredded cabbage

◁ **MAKES 36 MOMOS** ▷

If there is one dish that could represent Nepal, it would be their version of a dumpling known as *momo*. Made with Chinese dumpling wrappers, momos can be vegetarian or meat-filled and can be sealed a number of ways, including a pleated crescent shape (for beginners) or a round ball with a swirled top (the more traditional method—requiring skill). Here we steam the filled dumplings, but they can be pan-fried after steaming. (Eat Offbeat fries them for better transit.)

Paneer cheese can be found in the freezer section of international markets, but if you can't find it, you can easily make it at home (note that it will be softer than the store-bought equivalent). Ginger-garlic paste is a common condiment used in India and neighboring countries—you can find it online or at specialty grocers like Patel Brothers. A small bowl of sauce on the side is perfect for dipping. Rachana often tweaks her recipe for the dipping sauce; the version that appears here is a variation of her authentic tomato-based recipe, which takes much longer to prepare.

2 tablespoons olive oil, plus more for oiling the steamer

2 cups yellow onions, peeled and finely chopped

4 cups shredded cabbage

1 cup grated paneer cheese (homemade, page 121, or store-bought, see Note, page 120)

4 ounces cream cheese

2 tablespoons ghee

2 tablespoons ginger-garlic paste

½ teaspoon ground cardamom

½ teaspoon ground cinnamon

1 teaspoon kosher salt, or to taste

½ teaspoon freshly ground black pepper

½ teaspoon garam masala

1 teaspoon garlic powder

1 teaspoon onion powder

2 tablespoons finely chopped fresh cilantro leaves

36 round dumpling wrappers, defrosted (see page xix)

Savory Dipping Sauce (recipe follows), for serving

1   Heat the olive oil in a large sauté pan over medium heat. Once the oil is hot, add the onions and sauté until tender, about 5 minutes.

2   Working in batches if necessary to avoid crowding the pan, add the cabbage, paneer, cream cheese, and ghee. Cook, stirring occasionally, until the cabbage has softened slightly, 5 to 7 minutes. Remove the pan from the heat. Add the ginger-garlic paste, cardamom, cinnamon, salt, black pepper, garam masala, garlic powder, onion powder, and cilantro to the pan and stir.

3 For each momo, place a wrapper in your hand and put about 2 teaspoons of the filling in the middle. Fold the wrapper in half over the filling. Start at one edge and pinch the dough to seal at the corner. Seal by pinching a pleat into one edge and press the pleat against the opposite smooth edge. Continue to pleat and pinch to create a crescent-shaped dumpling with one smooth and one pleated side. Alternatively, gather the edge above the filling and pleat while twisting until sealed, creating a purse-shaped dumpling.

4 Lightly oil the inside of a bamboo steamer and place as many momos inside as can fit without crowding. Close the lid.

5 Place a pan big enough to hold the bamboo steamer over medium heat and add water to a depth of $1/2$ inch. Heat the water until it boils and then turn the heat down to low to maintain the steam. Place the bamboo steamer in the pan and steam the momos until cooked through, about 10 minutes.

6 Repeat Steps 4 and 5 with the remaining momos. Serve the momos immediately with a side of dipping sauce.

SAVORY DIPPING SAUCE

1 cup distilled white vinegar

1 cup sugar

¼ cup soy sauce

1 cup ketchup

1 teaspoon cornstarch

1 Place the vinegar, sugar, soy sauce, and ketchup in a small pot over medium heat. Bring to a boil, stirring, until the sugar is dissolved, about 5 minutes.

2 Combine the cornstarch and 1 tablespoon of water in a small bowl and whisk together with a fork. Stir into the sauce, then bring the sauce to a boil over high heat and boil until thickened, about 1 minute. Serve alongside the momos. Any extra sauce can be refrigerated in an airtight container for up to a week. Bring to room temperature before serving.

MOMOS WITH SPINACH FILLING

MAKES 30 MOMOS

Fresh spinach and paneer cheese is a common combination in South Asian cuisine. Here, the combo is turned into momo filling.

2 tablespoons olive oil

1 cup finely chopped yellow onion

1 tablespoon finely chopped fresh ginger

2 garlic cloves, peeled and finely chopped

1 teaspoon kosher salt, or to taste

16 ounces fresh spinach, triple-washed and drained, finely chopped

½ cup grated paneer cheese, (homemade, page 121, or store-bought, see Note, page 120)

30 round dumpling wrappers, defrosted (see page xix)

Savory Dipping Sauce (page 3), for serving

1   Heat the olive oil in a large sauté pan over medium heat. Once the oil is hot, add the onion, ginger, garlic, and salt. Sauté until the onion is tender, about 5 minutes. Add the spinach and cook until wilted, about 1 minute.

2   Transfer the spinach mixture to a medium mixing bowl and add the paneer. Carefully stir everything together. Let the mixture rest, covered, in the refrigerator for 15 minutes.

3   Once the mixture is cool, wrap and cook the momos as in Steps 3, 4, and 5 of the main recipe (page 3).

4   Serve the momos immediately with a side of dipping sauce.

MOMOS WITH CARROT AND GINGER FILLING

⟨ MAKES 36 MOMOS ⟩

Carrots and ginger are a lovely example of the flavors of the traditional Nepali table. This healthful vegetarian filling involves a quick sauté with cumin and ginger and a final touch of paneer cheese.

2 tablespoons olive oil

1 cup finely chopped yellow onion

2 tablespoons finely chopped fresh ginger

2 garlic cloves, peeled and minced

2 cups grated carrots

1 teaspoon ground cumin

1 teaspoon kosher salt, or to taste

½ cup grated paneer cheese, (homemade, page 121, or store-bought, see Note, page 120)

36 round dumpling wrappers, defrosted (see page xix)

Savory Dipping Sauce (page 3), for serving

1   Heat the olive oil in a sauté pan over medium heat. Once the oil is hot, add the onion, ginger, and garlic. Sauté until the onion is tender, about 5 minutes.

2   Stir in the carrots, cumin, and salt. Continue to sauté until the onion is fully cooked and the carrots are tender, about 5 minutes.

3   Transfer the onion and carrot mixture to a medium mixing bowl and add the paneer. Carefully stir everything together. Let the mixture rest, covered, in the refrigerator for 15 minutes.

4   Once the mixture is cool, wrap and cook the momos as in Steps 3, 4, and 5 of the main recipe (page 3).

5   Serve the momos immediately with a side of dipping sauce.

BEEF KIBBEH

Hand-shaped beef-and-bulgur croquettes with seven spices

◄ MAKES 22 KIBBEH ►

Kibbeh is a popular part of *mezze* (a selection of small plates served as appetizers) and street food cuisine from Egypt to Turkey. There are dozens of versions found throughout the region, and local variations can also be found in places with a large Levantine (aka eastern Mediterranean) population, like Mexico and Brazil. You want to make the final kibbeh into a football shape before frying it up. Diaa cups the meat mixture in one hand and uses the index finger of his other hand like a screwdriver to hollow out the insides for the filling. The kibbeh can be made a day ahead, if necessary. Just wrap them tightly in plastic wrap and keep them in the refrigerator until you are ready to fry. (They can also be made ahead and frozen, uncooked, for up to a week.)

It's hard to make this recipe without a meat grinder because the bulgur and ground beef need to be finely processed together. Diaa has been known to ask his butcher to prepare the ground mixture for him, so if you don't have the equipment to make this, try asking your local meat provider for assistance. (Don't try to use a food processor because this combination of ingredients can break the machine. Eat Offbeat knows from experience!)

1 cup fine bulgur	1½ cups finely chopped white onions	2 teaspoons freshly ground white pepper
¼ cup vegetable oil, plus more for deep-frying	2 pounds ground beef (80% lean)	1 tablespoon seven spices (see page xix)
	2 teaspoons kosher salt	

1 Place the bulgur in a large mixing bowl and add ½ cup of water. Soak it at room temperature until all the liquid is absorbed, 10 to 15 minutes.

2 Heat ¼ cup of the oil in a large sauté pan over medium heat. Once the oil is hot, add the onions and cook, stirring occasionally, until they are tender, about 7 minutes.

RECIPE CONTINUES

3 Add half of the ground beef, 1 teaspoon of the salt, 1 teaspoon of the white pepper, and the seven spices to the onions and cook, stirring every 5 minutes, until the beef has cooked through and browned, about 15 minutes.

4 Drain the beef filling in a colander to remove any excess oil. Transfer the filling to a medium mixing bowl and place it in the refrigerator, covered, until the beef has cooled, at least 20 minutes.

5 Add the remaining ground beef, 1 teaspoon of salt, and 1 teaspoon of white pepper to the soaked bulgur, and use your hands to mix it thoroughly.

6 Pass the beef-bulgur mixture through a meat grinder. Return it to the mixing bowl, add 1 cup of water, and thoroughly combine with your hands, kneading it a bit. Pass the mixture through the meat grinder once more—it should now resemble a dough.

7 Assemble the kibbeh: Take about 2 tablespoons of the bulgur mixture and form it into a ball in your hand. Hollow out the center with your index finger and place about 1 tablespoon of the cooked beef filling into the center. Carefully envelop the filling within the bulgur mixture, sealing the filling inside the bulgur shell. Once sealed, gently turn the sphere in your hands to create an oval football shape.

8 To fry the kibbeh, pour the remaining vegetable oil to a depth of at least 2 inches into a large stockpot or Dutch oven and clip a candy thermometer to the side, making sure it doesn't touch the bottom. Heat the oil to 375°F over high heat, then lower the heat to medium to maintain that temperature during frying. While the oil is heating up, line a large plate with paper towels.

9 Working in batches and using a slotted spoon or mesh strainer, place 8 to 10 kibbeh into the pot, without overcrowding. Fry the kibbeh until they are deep brown, 10 to 15 minutes. Carefully remove the finished kibbeh and place them on the towel-lined plate to absorb any excess oil. Serve immediately.

Hutchings, Shana Marie

Hold Slip
Franklin Ave. Library

10/28/21 01:22PM

Hold For: 255282

ITEM: 31704021021373
The kitchen without borders :
recipes and stories from
refugee and immigrant che

or: Hutchings, Shana Marie

ccount Balance Due 3.80

THE MANY WAYS OF KIBBEH

In Iraq, *kibbeh*—juicy bulgur and ground beef or lamb—is a festive food often included as an essential part of a mezze platter. The round balls of fried meat are so ubiquitous that there is a proverb about them. Dhuha, a chef from Iraq famous for her kibbeh-shaping technique, uses the phrase jokingly: *habbaya betsir Kubbaya*—literally "a ball out of a small grain," which translates loosely to "making a mountain out of a molehill," or *habbit el themmen bta'amel Kubba*, which means "a grain of rice becomes a kubba."

Kibbeh is ubiquitous throughout the Middle East. Its spelling permutations vary from *kubbeh* to *kebbe*, and there are many differences in preparation as well. The festive food can be fried, as it is in the Eat Offbeat kitchen, but also eaten raw, boiled, roasted, stewed, or baked into casseroles. It's a food that every family has a different way of making, and of course, everyone thinks their family recipe is the best. At Eat Offbeat, both Dhuha and Diaa, of Iraq and Syria, make the dish. Although their versions differ in shape and ingredients, both recipes are among the most popular on the kitchen's menu. For the two chefs, making kibbeh is a special skill passed down from a family member—Dhuha's from her mother, Diaa's from his uncle.

— POTATO KIBBEH —

Hand-shaped potato croquettes
stuffed with beef and herbs

◁ MAKES ABOUT 16 KIBBEH ▷

Although kibbeh is often made with bulgur, as in Diaa's recipe (page 7), Dhuha omits it and uses bread crumbs in a potato shell. When forming the kibbeh, try to create a flat disk around the filling.

4 russet potatoes (about 2½ pounds)	2 tablespoons vegetable oil, plus more for deep-frying	1 cup chopped fresh flat-leaf parsley leaves
2 tablespoons cornstarch	2 cups finely chopped yellow onions	5 teaspoons seven spices (see page xix)
2 tablespoons dried bread crumbs	1 pound ground beef (80% lean)	5 teaspoons ground cumin
4 teaspoons kosher salt	1½ teaspoons freshly ground black pepper	

1 Peel the potatoes, cut them into quarters, and place them in a large pot. Add water to cover the potatoes by 1 inch and bring to a boil over medium-high heat. Cook until fork-tender, about 15 minutes. Drain the potatoes, then return them to the pot. Add the cornstarch, bread crumbs, and 1 teaspoon of the salt. Mash the potatoes and stir to incorporate all the ingredients. Set aside.

2 Heat 2 tablespoons of the oil in a large nonstick skillet over medium heat. Once the oil is hot, add the onions and cook until soft and beginning to brown, about 10 minutes. Then add the ground beef, the remaining 3 teaspoons of salt, and the pepper, and cook until the meat is brown and cooked through, another 5 to 10 minutes.

3 Remove the pan from the heat and let the beef mixture cool slightly. If there's any excess oil in the skillet, drain the beef mixture in a colander to remove the fat, then add the parsley, seven spices, and cumin and stir to combine.

RECIPE CONTINUES

4 Assemble the kibbeh: Take about 2 tablespoons of the potato mixture and form it into a flat disk in your hand. Place about 1 tablespoon of the meat filling in the center. Carefully envelop the filling within the potato shell, sealing the filling inside. Once sealed, gently flatten the sphere into a small disk. Set aside. Kibbeh can be made ahead and frozen, uncooked, for up to a week.

5 To fry the kibbeh, pour the remaining vegetable oil to a depth of at least 2 inches into a large stockpot or Dutch oven and clip a candy thermometer to the side, making sure it doesn't touch the bottom. Heat the oil to 375°F over high heat, then lower the heat to medium to maintain that temperature during frying. While the oil is heating up, line a large plate with paper towels.

6 Working in batches and taking care not to overcrowd the pot, slowly lower 3 or 4 kibbeh into the oil, using a slotted spoon. Fry the kibbeh until they are deep golden brown, 7 to 8 minutes. Remove with a mesh strainer and place them on the towel-lined plate to absorb any excess oil. Allow the oil to return to 375°F in between batches, if necessary.

7 Let the kibbeh cool for about 15 minutes. Serve warm.

FATAYER

Hand pies stuffed with chicken, peppers,
pomegranate molasses, and Cheddar

◅ MAKES 24 FATAYER ▻

Fatayer are the Middle East's version of meat-filled hand pies. Common throughout the region, they can be stuffed with anything from feta to spinach and Swiss chard to the chicken, bell peppers, and Cheddar cheese in Dhuha's version. The fatayer can be sealed in semicircles, as they are in the Eat Offbeat kitchen, or they can be folded into triangles similar to *hamantaschen*, the filled cookie associated with the Jewish holiday of Purim.

Dhuha is adamant—these hand pies do not need sauce! They should be juicy enough as is. However, she says, some people do like to serve fatayer with a yogurt dip (pictured on page 15) made of cucumber and garlic or tahini and lemon. Others bake the fatayer instead of frying them. If you want a healthier version, brush the fatayer on both sides with oil, then bake them at 350°F until golden brown, about 20 minutes.

---

1 pound boneless, skinless chicken breasts

3 tablespoons canola oil

1 cup thinly sliced yellow onion

2 teaspoons freshly ground black pepper

1½ teaspoons kosher salt

⅓ cup finely chopped red bell pepper

⅓ cup finely chopped orange bell pepper

⅓ cup finely chopped yellow bell pepper

8 ounces cremini or button mushrooms, trimmed and finely chopped

1 tablespoon fresh lemon juice

2 tablespoons pomegranate molasses (see page xviii)

2½ teaspoons ground sumac (see page xix)

2½ teaspoons ground cardamom

2½ teaspoons seven spices (see page xix)

1 tablespoon ground cumin

14 ounces grated Cheddar cheese

24 empanada wrappers (see page xix)

Vegetable oil, for deep-frying

---

1   Cut the chicken breasts into 1-inch cubes.

2   Heat the canola oil in a large pot over medium heat. Once the oil is hot, add the onion and lightly sauté until it's softened, about 2 minutes. Add the chicken cubes,

RECIPE CONTINUES

black pepper, and salt. Continue sautéing until the chicken is no longer pink on the outside, about 5 minutes. Then stir in the red, orange, and yellow bell peppers and cook until the peppers are tender, about 5 minutes more.

3 Stir in the mushrooms, lemon juice, and pomegranate molasses. Cook until the mushrooms are tender, about 5 minutes, then add the sumac, cardamom, seven spices, and cumin. Cook until the spices infuse the mushroom mixture, about 2 minutes more. Remove the pot from the heat.

4 While the filling is still hot, stir in the Cheddar cheese. Once all of the cheese has melted, let the filling cool in the refrigerator for 20 minutes.

5 Assemble the fatayer: Take an empanada wrapper in one hand and place 2 tablespoons of filling in the center. Fold the wrapper in half over the filling, pinching to seal the edges together. Use a dab of water along the edges, if necessary. Repeat until the filling is used up.

6 To fry the fatayer, pour the vegetable oil to a depth of at least 2 inches into a large stockpot or Dutch oven and clip a candy thermometer to the side, making sure it doesn't touch the bottom. Heat the oil to 375°F over high heat, then lower the heat to medium to maintain that temperature during frying. While the oil is heating up, line a large plate with paper towels.

7 Working in batches and taking care not to overcrowd the pot, slowly lower 3 or 4 fatayer into the oil using a slotted spoon. Fry them until they are deep golden brown, about 10 minutes. Remove them with a mesh strainer and place them on the towel-lined plate. Bring the oil back to 375°F between batches, if necessary. Repeat with the rest of the fatayer, then serve immediately.

— SAMOSAS —

Fried hand pies with spiced potato filling

MAKES ABOUT 24 SAMOSAS WITH EMPANADA WRAPPERS, OR 30 WITH PHYLLO DOUGH

Fried samosas filled with savory potatoes and other vegetables are a staple of Indian menus around the world, so this Nepali version may feel familiar. Although these are fried in the catering kitchen, you can easily bake them for an alternative: Brush one side of each samosa with egg white or milk, and place them in a 350°F oven until the tops are golden brown, about 20 minutes. Carefully flip the samosas, brush the other side with egg white or milk, and return them to the oven to get that golden brown on the remaining side, about 10 minutes more.

2 pounds russet potatoes, peeled and quartered

¼ cup vegetable oil, plus more for deep-frying

1 teaspoon cumin seeds

1 teaspoon coriander seeds

2 cups fresh or frozen green peas

2 bird's-eye chiles, finely diced (see page xvii)

1 tablespoon minced garlic

1 teaspoon ground turmeric

1 teaspoon ground cumin

1 teaspoon garam masala

6 medium yellow onions, peeled and finely chopped

⅓ cup fresh cilantro leaves

24 empanada wrappers (see page xix), defrosted, or 8 ounces phyllo dough

Flour, for dusting (if using empanada wrappers)

6 tablespoons melted ghee (if using phyllo dough)

1   Bring a large pot of water to a boil over high heat. Place the potatoes in the pot, return the water to a boil, lower the heat to medium, and cook the potatoes until fork-tender, about 10 minutes. Drain the potatoes, place them in a large mixing bowl, and lightly mash them with a fork, leaving some small chunks if you like more texture.

2   Heat ¼ cup of the oil in a medium nonstick skillet over medium heat. When the oil is hot, add the cumin seeds and coriander seeds, sautéing them until slightly toasted and aromatic, about 1 minute. Add the peas and chiles, sautéing them until tender, about 5 minutes. Stir in the garlic, turmeric, cumin, and garam masala. Continue cooking until everything is tender, about 5 minutes, and then add the onions. Cook until the onions are translucent and everything else is browned, 5 to 7 minutes. Remove the pan from the heat.

3 Add the pea mixture and the cilantro to the potatoes and stir to combine thoroughly. Set aside to cool.

4 *If using empanada wrappers*, place 1 wrapper on a well-floured surface and roll it out into a thin oval. Place 3 tablespoons of the filling on the bottom half of the wrapper. Fold the bottom edge of the wrapper left to right to form a triangular pocket over the filling. Continue to fold the triangle until all the wrapper is used up. Seal the edges with water. Set the samosa aside on a platter. Repeat until the filling is gone.

If using phyllo dough, place 1 sheet of the dough, horizontally oriented, on a floured surface. (Roll the other phyllo sheets back up and place them under a damp cloth to keep them from drying out.) Brush melted ghee on the right half of the sheet. Fold the left side over it, like closing a book, so that the ghee holds the two sides together. Cut the sheet vertically into two long rectangles. Place 2 tablespoons of filling on a bottom corner of one rectangle. Fold the bottom edge up and toward the other side to enclose the filling and form a triangle. Continue folding the triangle up the length of the rectangle to encase the filling in several layers of dough. Tuck the final flap of dough over the top and seal the edges with water. Set the samosa aside on a platter. Repeat until the filling is gone.

5 To fry the samosas, pour vegetable oil to a depth of at least 2 inches into a large stockpot or Dutch oven and clip a candy thermometer to the side, making sure it doesn't touch the bottom. Heat the oil to 375°F over high heat, then lower the heat to medium to maintain that temperature during frying. While the oil is heating up, line a large plate with paper towels.

6 Using a slotted spoon or fine mesh strainer, place 4 or 5 samosas into the pot, without overcrowding. Fry the samosas until golden brown, about 10 minutes for empanada wrappers or 15 minutes for phyllo dough. Carefully remove the samosas and place them on the towel-lined plate to absorb any excess oil. Repeat with the remaining samosas.

7 Let cool for about 15 minutes before serving.

CHEF HÉCTOR ✳ VENEZUELA

CACHAPAS

Corn cakes topped with melted butter and cheese

⟨ **MAKES 4 CACHAPAS** ⟩

Cachapas are a popular street food in Venezuela—though the authentic preparation is slightly different, they are easily adapted. The corn kernels are ground but left slightly coarse, so the finished pancakes taste, well, corny. Any leftover kernels can be cooked and added as garnish. The sweet corn cakes are topped with butter and any kind of cheese that melts, from queso fresco to mozzarella. If you simply want to try something more breakfast-like, they can be topped with butter alone. Héctor serves these for breakfast with *nata* (crème fraîche) and feta cheese on the side, or for lunch with the Hearts of Palm Salad (page 54).

3 cups uncooked corn kernels, scraped from their cobs, or frozen and defrosted

1 cup unbleached all-purpose flour

1 large egg

1 tablespoon kosher salt

2 tablespoons sugar

2 tablespoons unsalted butter

6 ounces crème fraîche or other cheese, such as crumbled queso fresco or grated mozzarella

Cooked corn kernels, for garnish (optional)

1 serrano pepper, sliced, for garnish (optional)

1   Place the uncooked corn kernels in a food processor and pulse to form a somewhat coarse puree, about 1 minute. Strain out the juice and place the puree in a medium mixing bowl.

2   Add the flour, egg, salt, and sugar to the corn puree, and whisk until well combined to make the cachapa batter.

3   Melt 1 teaspoon of the butter in a large nonstick skillet over medium-high heat. Working in batches, spoon a scant cup of cachapa batter into the pan to form a pancake. Cook until the bottom is golden, 4 to 5 minutes. Flip and cook the other side, 4 to 5 minutes more. Set aside the finished cachapa and repeat with the rest of the batter, adding teaspoons of butter to the pan as needed.

4   Serve stacked or folded in half with the remaining butter and crème fraîche. Add the cooked corn and sliced serrano, if desired.

KUKU SABZI

Persian herbed frittata

SERVES 6 AS AN APPETIZER

Although it may translate as such to Western audiences, calling *kuku sabzi* a frittata is doing it a disservice. The stars of this dish are the herbs; the eggs simply hold everything together. Green garlic—young garlic with tender leaves and a milder flavor than the bulbs—can be found at farmers' markets in early spring. The *zereshk* (barberries) add a nice tangy component. If you can't find them, dried red currants or unsweetened cranberries—chopped, if they aren't very small—can be used in a pinch.

Cooking spray, for greasing the pan

6 cups fresh flat-leaf parsley leaves

2 cups fresh cilantro leaves

2 cups fresh dill fronds

½ cup shelled walnuts

3 garlic cloves, peeled and minced (Nasrin uses green garlic)

2 teaspoons ground turmeric

1 teaspoon kosher salt

1 teaspoon freshly ground black pepper

¼ cup dried zereshk (barberries; see page xix), plus more for garnish

6 large eggs, lightly beaten

1 Preheat the oven to 350°F. Spray a 10-inch round cake pan with cooking spray and line it with parchment paper.

2 Finely chop the parsley, cilantro, and dill. Coarsely chop the walnuts.

3 Place the herbs, walnuts, garlic, turmeric, salt, pepper, and zereshk in a medium mixing bowl and stir to combine.

4 Add the eggs to the bowl and fold them in to coat the filling.

5 Pour the mixture into the prepared pan. Bake until the eggs are set, 20 to 25 minutes.

6 Sprinkle a few zereshk over the top, if desired, cut into wedges, and serve immediately.

─ HUMMUS ─

Chickpea dip with tahini and lemon

Hummus was the recipe that started Eat Offbeat. When co-founder Manal first moved to the States, she could not find any version available in New York City that came close to her family's recipe, so she started to make and serve the version passed down from her grandmother. Though it's ubiquitous, hummus is a very contentious food—this recipe is the one that Manal likes best. Some purists may suggest that you peel the chickpeas to get a smoother, whiter consistency, but Manal's grandmother claims all the nutrients are locked in the skins. Process this hummus until it's silky smooth and serve with fresh pita.

1 cup dried chickpeas

5 garlic cloves, peeled and roughly chopped

3 tablespoons lemon juice

1 tablespoon extra virgin olive oil, plus more for serving

¾ cup tahini

2 teaspoons kosher salt, plus more as needed

2 tablespoons plain yogurt

A pinch of ground cumin, plus more for garnish

Ground paprika, for garnish

1 Place the chickpeas in a medium bowl and add water to cover. Let soak 6 to 8 hours, then drain.

2 Place the chickpeas in a large pot and cover them with fresh water. Set the pot over medium-high heat and simmer until the chickpeas are soft but not yet mushy, at least 30 minutes. Drain the chickpeas.

3 Reserve a few cooked chickpeas for garnish, if desired. Place the remaining chickpeas, garlic, lemon juice, olive oil, tahini, salt, yogurt, and a pinch of cumin in a food processor. Pulse until blended and creamy, about 30 seconds. Add more salt to taste, if desired.

4 Serve with a dusting of cumin and/or paprika, a drizzle of olive oil, and any reserved cooked chickpeas on top.

CHEF NASRIN

IRAN

THOUGH SHE HAILS FROM TEHRAN, ANOTHER BIG CITY, NASRIN REJALI admits to being overwhelmed when she first arrived in New York. After a two-year stay in Turkey, she was granted refugee status and sent to the New York area since her brother—and sponsor—was nearby. Resettlement proved tough for a variety of reasons, but her children and Eat Offbeat helped her come to love her new home.

Cooking comes naturally to Nasrin. Her main teachers were her mother, Ferdous, and her paternal grandmother. When she was growing up, both households were always hubbubs of activity, with parties and friends stopping by and everyone always ready to eat. When she was about ten years old, she declared to her mother that she would make the traditional Iranian dish *ghormeh sabzi* for her visiting aunt and cousin. Ghormeh sabzi—a stew made of herbs, meat, and beans—is one of the dishes for which every Persian household has its own recipe, handed down through the generations. Nasrin's family was no exception, and it often graced their table. Once the ghormeh sabzi was done, young Nasrin presented the entrée to everyone, nervous about their reaction. Much to her relatives' surprise, her first time cooking for her family was a success.

> **"WHEN THE COOKS ARE TWO, THE FOOD IS EITHER SALTY OR BLAND."**
> —IRANIAN PROVERB

Her favorite dish, though, has always been *fesenjan*, a dish laced with pomegranate syrup and thickened with ground walnuts. It's traditionally made with chicken, but Nasrin prefers it with ground beef. Her grandmother made her delicious version of fesenjan every year for Nasrin's birthday. Finally, when she was thirty, after years of watching her grandmother mix the walnuts and chop the onions, Nasrin felt ready to make it for her grandmother, who lived with her at the time. "Afterward my grandmother said to me, 'Yours is better!'" even though all the ingredients and processes were the same. Nasrin's love for the dish comes through whenever she makes fesenjan. Soon after Nasrin's first success, her grandmother was diagnosed with terminal cancer, and Nasrin had to take care of her, feeding her all the dishes her grandmother had taught her how to cook. Now,

Nasrin thinks of her grandmother when cooking, "for all the recipes she gave me with love."

Cooking those dishes helped ground her while she was sorting out her life in New York. At one point, Nasrin and her children lived in a hotel room while she worked two jobs to make ends meet. Having just started at Eat Offbeat, she would bring food back there from the Eat Offbeat kitchen, something to remind her family of home. Once they were situated in an apartment, Nasrin's daughter, Armita, could help in the kitchen at home, perfecting her own versions of ghormeh sabzi and fesenjan while Nasrin went to work. Her oldest son, Armin, sometimes picks up an Eat Offbeat shift when there are hundreds of momos to be folded or meatballs to be rolled.

Now, Nasrin is working full-time at Eat Offbeat, and she couldn't be happier. For her, the work is more than just preparing trays of food for catering customers—it's directly interacting with strangers through the creation of each dish. She misses the feeling of having family all together in one place, so she famously hosts parties in her house—once she fit at least thirty-five people in her small dining room, when she hosted the Eat Offbeat staff. Her dream is to create a space where all people can come to eat, relax, and be happy, and, as she says, *noshe jan* (enjoy). There are no walls or barriers when Nasrin is cooking with such love.

A NOTE FROM NASRIN ON INTERNATIONAL REFUGEE DAY, 2019

For people who once left their homes, memories, joys, fathers, mothers, loved ones on the streets, they went somewhere else in the world to make life a little easier . . . a trip that is not always safe, and in many cases, a trip from which there is no return.

Immigrants see every night in their dreams their homes—and the shops where they used to go and hear the laughs of their beloved. Many of them still think in the morning of the smell of the freshly baked bread from the towns . . . the smell of bread that does not exist now.

I am hoping for a day when nobody in the world has to leave home for any reason.

— MIRZA GHASEMI —

Charred eggplant dip
with stewed tomatoes, onion, and garlic

◅ SERVES 4 TO 6 AS AN APPETIZER ▻

Mirza ghasemi is an eggplant-based dip from northern Iran that tends to show up in mezze or as an appetizer. It is usually made with eggs, though Nasrin often makes it without for a vegan version. Cooking the eggplant is a little messy, but Nasrin refuses to make it in the oven—if you don't have a gas range, try using an outdoor grill instead. Serve this with crackers, flatbread, or pita as part of a spread.

2 medium eggplants (about 2 pounds)

1 can (28 ounces) whole tomatoes

10 garlic cloves, peeled

2 tablespoons olive oil

2 cups finely chopped red onions, plus more for garnish

1 teaspoon kosher salt

2 teaspoons freshly ground black pepper

2 teaspoons ground turmeric

2 plum tomatoes, seeded and diced

2 large eggs

Sprig of mint, for garnish (optional)

1 Turn the gas to high and place one eggplant directly on the grate. Cook it until the skin cracks and turns very dark, 5 to 10 minutes. Flip the eggplant and char the other side, 5 to 10 minutes more. Set the eggplant aside to cool and repeat with the second eggplant. When the eggplants are cool enough to touch, remove the skin, or cut them open and scoop out the mushy insides and set aside.

2 Puree the canned tomatoes with their juices and the garlic in a blender at low speed, about 2 minutes. Set aside.

3 Heat the olive oil in a large nonstick skillet over medium heat. Add the 2 cups of onion and cook, stirring frequently, until it is translucent, about 5 minutes.

4 Stir in the salt, black pepper, and turmeric to incorporate the spices. Continue to cook for 1 minute more, then stir in the diced plum tomatoes and cook until they are tender and broken down, 2 to 3 minutes.

5 Stir in the eggplant, then stir in the tomato-and-garlic puree. Lower the heat to medium-low and continue to cook, stirring frequently, until the sauce has thickened, about 10 minutes.

6 Beat the eggs in a small bowl. Stir ¼ cup of the hot eggplant-tomato mixture into the beaten eggs to warm them. Quickly pour the eggs into the rest of the eggplant-tomato sauce in the skillet, mixing thoroughly until the eggs are cooked and the sauce has turned orange, about 5 minutes.

7 Serve the dip topped with red onion and a sprig of mint, if desired.

GETTING THAT SMOKY EGGPLANT FLAVOR

There are many ways to char an eggplant, but for Nasrin's Mirza Ghasemi and Kashk Bademjan (page 30), a gas stove is imperative. If you don't have a gas range, an outdoor grill works just as well, but don't use the oven—even though it's possible to char eggplant under the broiler or cook it on a grill pan, Nasrin says the taste is not as good. However, for Dhuha's Baba Ghannoush (page 33), using the oven is slightly more acceptable, which is why you'll find an oven technique there.

KASHK BADEMJAN

Turmeric-spiced eggplant and onion dip

SERVES 6 TO 8 AS AN APPETIZER

The base of this easy dip is roasted eggplant. It's built upon with walnuts, tender onions, and dried mint. But it's made into a dish with *kashk bibi*, or Persian fermented whey. The tangy ingredient is found in the dairy section of international grocery stores and specialty markets. If you can't find it, sour cream can be a passable substitute. Depending on what blend of turmeric you use, this dish may range in color from brown to yellow.

2 medium eggplants (about 2 pounds)

4 tablespoons olive oil

1 cup shelled walnuts

1 cup finely chopped white onion

4 teaspoons ground turmeric

1½ teaspoons freshly ground black pepper

2 plum tomatoes, peeled and diced

1 teaspoon kosher salt

¾ cup dried mint

¾ cup kashk bibi (see page xviii), plus more for serving

1 Turn the gas to high and place one eggplant directly on the grate. Cook it until the skin cracks and turns very dark, 5 to 10 minutes. Flip the eggplant and char the other side, 5 to 10 minutes more. Set the eggplant aside to cool. When the eggplant is cool enough to touch, remove the skin, or cut it open and scoop out the mushy insides and set aside.

2 Line a plate with paper towels. Peel the other eggplant and cut it into thick slices. Heat 1 tablespoon of the olive oil in a large nonstick skillet over medium-high heat. Once the oil is hot, carefully place the eggplant slices into the skillet and pan-fry until golden brown, 4 to 5 minutes per side. Remove the browned slices from the heat and place them on the towel-lined plate to cool.

3 Place the grilled eggplant and eggplant slices in a food processor. Add the walnuts and pulse until smooth, about 1 minute. Set aside.

RECIPE CONTINUES

4   Heat another tablespoon of the olive oil in the nonstick skillet over medium heat. When the oil is hot, add the onion and sauté until translucent, about 5 minutes. Stir in the turmeric and pepper, thoroughly coating the onion. Cook until the spices are fragrant, about 2 minutes. Stir in the plum tomatoes and the salt and lower the heat to medium-low. Continue to cook, stirring, until the tomatoes begin to soften, about 3 minutes. Remove the pan from the heat.

5   Pour the tomato-onion mixture into a medium mixing bowl. Stir in the eggplant-walnut puree, ⅓ cup of the dried mint, and the kashk bibi. Mix until combined.

6   Pour the remaining 2 tablespoons of olive oil into a small nonstick skillet and place over medium-high heat. When the oil is hot, stir in the rest of the dried mint and fry until crunchy, 30 seconds to 1 minute. Remove the pan from the heat.

7   Spoon the kashk bademjan into a large bowl, topping with more spoonfuls of kashk bibi, and sprinkle to taste with the crunchy dried mint. Serve immediately.

BABA GHANNOUSH

Roasted eggplant dip with tahini

SERVES 4 TO 6 AS AN APPETIZER

Baba Ghannoush is one of the Middle East's most famous dips. Roasted eggplants, yogurt, and tahini come together to form a creamy dip that works with anything from crackers to triangles of pita to crudités. Many cooks choose to grill the eggplants directly over a medium flame on the gas stove, flipping each eggplant often, until the skin blackens and chars (see box on page 29). This method gives Baba Ghannoush a smokier taste that is unique to the dip. The oven version is much easier for larger volumes, which is why it is included here, but the authentic method is on the stove. Store leftovers in an airtight container in the refrigerator for up to 5 days. Bring the dip to room temperature before serving.

2 medium eggplants (about 2 pounds)

½ cup plain yogurt

¼ cup tahini

2 garlic cloves, peeled

1 teaspoon kosher salt

1½ teaspoons extra virgin olive oil, for serving

1 Preheat the oven to 400°F. Line a sheet pan with parchment paper.

2 Poke holes in the eggplants with a fork and place them on the prepared sheet pan. Roast until they are very tender and can be easily pierced with a toothpick, about 1 hour. Remove from the oven and let cool.

3 Once the eggplants are cool enough to handle, spoon out the insides and discard the skins.

4 Place the eggplant, yogurt, tahini, garlic, and salt in a food processor. Pulse until the mixture becomes a smooth puree, about 30 seconds.

5 Serve drizzled with olive oil.

CHEF DHUHA

IRAQ

AT THE CENTER OF THE MIDDLE EAST AND THE HOME OF NUMEROUS ANCIENT civilizations (and, some theorize, the world's first cookbooks), Iraq is both unique in its food culture and heavily influenced by the surrounding region. The country's ties to Islam play out significantly in its cuisine and traditions.

For Dhuha Jasim, not many days stand out in her memories of cooking with her mother, Sajde, in Baghdad, Iraq, because she grew up in the kitchen, helping her mother cook for the family of seven. But there are a few special moments that she recalls, like when she was learning to make Potato Kibbeh (page 11) for the first time. She shaped a couple of kibbeh, putting them aside for Sajde's inspection but knowing full well that her mother was a bit of a perfectionist. The shape was off and into the trash they went. Dhuha made six more. Those too went right in the garbage. It wasn't until around her fifteenth attempt that they were deemed passable—a short learning curve for someone who'd watched her mother mold kibbeh for years.

Learning how to make Potato Kibbeh might be a highlight of Dhuha's food memories because of the dish's significance: It's a pillar of Ramadan and Eid al-Fitr menus. Prior to the month of religious fasting, Muslim households will prepare and freeze a substantial amount of food for the daily sunset meal, or *iftar*. In Dhuha's family, every iftar includes a lentil soup, rice, and a variety of freshly fried kibbeh (in addition to the potato version).

For Eid al-Fitr, the holiday at the end of Ramadan, a great number of sweets, including numerous baklava, are prepared. But Dhuha admits that she didn't truly learn how to make baklava until she arrived in the United States. In Iraq and much of the Middle East, baklava is usually bought from professional bakeries that roll out their own phyllo dough and craft the dessert into elegant shapes. Unimpressed by the overly sweet and cinnamon-flavored versions found in the New York area, Dhuha began making her own (page 194) for family celebrations, versions that rang true to her Iraqi culture. And like many religious festivities tend to do, the meals and preparation she undertakes for Ramadan and Eid al-Fitr give her a chance to pass down her recipes to her two sons.

CHEF NASRIN ✳ IRAN

─ BORANI ESFENAJ ─

Creamy spinach dip

◄ MAKES 4 SERVINGS AS AN APPETIZER ►

Borani Esfenaj is a traditional Persian appetizer that's at home next to other spreads such as baba ghannoush and hummus. Nasrin's version includes mint and basil, making it the perfect cooling dip for summer meals on hot days.

1 pound fresh spinach, triple-washed and drained

¼ cup fresh mint leaves

1 cup fresh basil leaves

¼ cup shelled walnuts

2 garlic cloves, peeled

2 teaspoons kosher salt

1 teaspoon freshly ground black pepper

2 cups Greek yogurt

½ cup dried mint, plus more for garnish

1   Place a large nonstick skillet over medium heat. Once it is warm, add the spinach and cook until it wilts, about 3 minutes. Remove the pan from the heat.

2   Place the fresh mint, basil, walnuts, and garlic in a food processor. Pulse until a paste is formed, about 30 seconds. Add the salt and pepper and pulse a couple of times. Add the yogurt and pulse until fully incorporated, about 30 more seconds.

3   Place the wilted spinach and dried mint in a small mixing bowl. Pour in the yogurt sauce and gently stir to coat the spinach. Sprinkle with a pinch of dried mint for garnish and serve immediately.

THE ULTIMATE FAMILY MEAL

Mezze (also known as *meze* or *maza*) permeates the cuisines of all nations that belonged to the former Ottoman Empire, including Greece and the Balkans. Originating from the Persian word *maze* ("taste" or "snack"), mezze consists of small plates that are served either at once or in succession, with cold dishes preceding hot ones. Despite the strong resemblance to hors d'oeuvres, Middle Eastern cultures tend to view mezze as a primary course rather than a prelude. It is capable of being the entire meal and is often eaten this way; therefore, a more fitting parallel may be the smörgåsbord, the Scandinavian buffet-style meal that has entered the English lexicon.

Elements of mezze platters vary culturally and regionally. In Mediterranean territories, alcoholic beverages such as wine and anise-based liqueur are enjoyed alongside mezze. Here, the dishes are treated as snacks as opposed to a meal. In Levantine countries, mezze sometimes takes on a similar role—sans alcohol—that is known as *muqabbilat*, Arabic for "starters."

Mezze's emphasis on togetherness transcends geographic variances. Sharing, serving, and passing an abundance of small plates among family and friends creates community. To create your own, gather the following items as a spread: mixed olives, labneh, raw garden vegetables, fresh mint, lettuce, cabbage, Musabbaha (page 39), Hummus (page 23), Baba Ghannoush (page 33), Mirza Ghasemi (page 28), Kashk Bademjan (page 30), Tabbouleh (page 57), and Kibbeh (pages 7 and 11).

MUSABBAHA

Tahini-dressed chickpea salad

SERVES 4 TO 6 AS AN APPETIZER

Found in dishes like hummus and falafel, chickpeas are a staple legume throughout the Middle East. If you're a fan of the former, you'll love *musabbaha*. The dish resembles a "deconstructed" hummus where the chickpeas are kept whole. It can be eaten as a side salad or served as a dip with pita and chips.

¾ cup Greek yogurt

¼ cup tahini

2 tablespoons fresh lemon juice

3½ cups cooked chickpeas (about 30 ounces canned), drained

⅓ cup thinly sliced red onion

1 teaspoon kosher salt

1 teaspoon freshly ground black pepper

1½ cups finely chopped fresh flat-leaf parsley leaves

½ cup diced tomato

4 teaspoons extra virgin olive oil

1 Place the yogurt, tahini, and lemon juice in a large mixing bowl and whisk until fully combined. Stir in the chickpeas, red onion, salt, and pepper.

2 Spoon the chickpea mixture into a shallow bowl. Scatter the parsley and tomato over the top and drizzle with the olive oil. Serve at room temperature or after chilling in the refrigerator for 2 hours.

ZEYTOON PARVARDEH

Olive, pomegranate, and walnut tapenade

⊰ SERVES 4 AS AN APPETIZER ⊱

This traditional Persian appetizer hails from the northern part of Iran. Golpar powder, also know as Angelica powder, is an aromatic Persian spice made of ground seeds—often sprinkled over fava beans. The spice can be found at specialty grocers or online, as can pomegranate molasses. The latter is pomegranate juice that has been reduced to syrup—and it's often made without adding any sugar.

½ cup shelled walnuts

1 tablespoon fresh mint leaves

1 teaspoon golpar powder (optional; see headnote)

½ cup plain yogurt

2 jars (8 ounces each) whole pitted green olives, drained

1 tablespoon pomegranate molasses (see page xviii)

Kosher salt and freshly ground black pepper

1 cup fresh pomegranate seeds (see box on page 137)

1 Place the walnuts, fresh mint, golpar powder, if using, and yogurt in a food processor. Pulse until a paste is formed, about 30 seconds.

2 Transfer the paste to a medium mixing bowl and add the olives, stirring until they are thoroughly coated. Then stir in the pomegranate molasses and add salt and pepper to taste. Serve topped with fresh pomegranate seeds.

SALADS
AND
SOUPS

SUMAC SALAD

*Fresh cucumber and tomato salad
in lemon-sumac vinaigrette*

— 44 —

SALAD SHIRAZI

*Fresh cucumber, tomato, and feta
in lime-mint dressing*

— 45 —

EDAMAME SALAD

*Edamame, shredded cabbage, tomato,
and mint salad with cider vinaigrette*

— 46 —

FATTOUSH

*Fresh lettuce, tomato, cucumber, and onion
in lemon and olive oil with crispy pita*

— 52 —

HEARTS OF PALM SALAD

*Hearts of palm and avocado
in a simple vinaigrette*

— 54 —

KATAHAR SALAD

*Shredded jackfruit with fresh tomato and
cucumber in lemon-cilantro dressing*

— 55 —

TABBOULEH SALAD

*Mint-scented parsley salad
with fresh tomato, onion, and bulgur
in lemon–olive oil dressing*

— 57 —

LENTIL SOUP

*Warming black lentil soup
in jimbu-flavored spicy broth*

— 58 —

RED PEPPER SOUP

*Pureed red bell peppers
with brioche croutons*

— 63 —

MA'AREENA SOUP

*Spaghetti and tomato soup
with ground beef and mozzarella*

— 64 —

— SUMAC SALAD —

Fresh cucumber and tomato salad
in lemon-sumac vinaigrette

◁ SERVES 4 TO 6 AS A SIDE SALAD ▷

A combination of tomatoes, red onions, and cucumbers always makes a cooling summer salad. But this one gets a special kick from tangy ground sumac. The purple spice is a popular ingredient in the Middle East, but the shrub is found throughout North America and Asia as well. When Eat Offbeat needed a refreshing salad to add to their menu, Dhuha immediately thought of this traditional dish. Sometimes she adds a little bit of pomegranate molasses to the dressing to give the flavor a boost of that unmistakable tangy sweetness.

2 cups diced tomatoes

2 cups diced cucumbers

½ cup diced red onion

½ cup ground sumac
(see page xix)

½ cup finely chopped fresh
flat-leaf parsley leaves

½ cup extra virgin olive oil

2 teaspoons kosher salt

¼ cup fresh lemon juice

¼ cup distilled white vinegar

1 tablespoon pomegranate
molasses (optional; see page xviii)

1   Place the tomatoes, cucumbers, onion, ¼ cup of the sumac, and the parsley in a medium mixing bowl.

2   Place the olive oil, salt, lemon juice, vinegar, pomegranate molasses, if using, and remaining ¼ cup of sumac in a small mixing bowl and whisk to combine.

3   Pour the dressing over the vegetables and gently fold until the salad is thoroughly coated. Serve.

SALAD SHIRAZI

Fresh cucumber, tomato,
and feta in lime-mint dressing

SERVES 4 AS A SIDE SALAD

A fresh salad of tomatoes, cucumber, red onion, and feta is perfect during summer's vegetable bounty. Nasrin's version involves dried mint leaves to bring a pop of green and a bright element to your usual side.

2 plum tomatoes, seeded and diced	½ red onion, peeled and diced	Juice of 1 lime
1 large cucumber, diced	1 cup dried mint	2 teaspoons kosher salt
	¼ cup extra virgin olive oil	4 ounces feta cheese

1 Place the tomatoes, cucumber, and onion in a medium mixing bowl and stir in the dried mint.

2 Place the olive oil, lime juice, and salt in a small bowl and whisk to combine. Pour the dressing over the salad and stir to coat.

3 Crumble the feta over the salad and serve.

CHEF RACHANA ✳ NEPAL

EDAMAME SALAD

*Edamame, shredded cabbage, tomato,
and mint salad with cider vinaigrette*

SERVES 6 AS A SIDE SALAD

Usually found as a pre-sushi appetizer, edamame is a focal point of this green cabbage salad. The cider vinegar–based dressing tenderizes the cabbage, but don't let it sit too long—you want it to maintain a good crunch. Like any well-planned salad, the dish comes together quickly once all the chopping is done.

½ head green cabbage (about 1 pound), outer leaves removed

2 tablespoons kosher salt

12 ounces frozen shelled edamame

⅓ cup apple cider vinegar

⅓ cup fresh lemon juice

⅓ cup extra virgin olive oil

1½ teaspoons freshly ground black pepper

1 tablespoon dried mint

1½ teaspoons ground cumin

1 teaspoon ground coriander

½ teaspoon ground cardamom

1 teaspoon ground ginger

1 teaspoon garlic powder

½ teaspoon ground cinnamon

2 cups diced plum tomatoes

2 cups diced cucumber

2 tablespoons chopped fresh cilantro leaves

1 Core the cabbage and slice into thin strips. You should end up with about 4 cups of shredded cabbage.

2 Fill a medium pot with water and bring it to a boil over high heat. Add 1 tablespoon of the salt to the water and bring it to a boil again.

3 Add the edamame to the pot and boil until the beans are al dente but still bright green, about 8 minutes. Drain and rinse with cool water.

4 Place the cider vinegar, lemon juice, olive oil, remaining 1 tablespoon of salt, and the pepper in a large mixing bowl and whisk until emulsified. Whisk in the dried mint, cumin, coriander, cardamom, ginger, garlic powder, and cinnamon until fully incorporated.

5 Add the cabbage, edamame, tomatoes, cucumber, and cilantro to the bowl and carefully fold to coat with the dressing. Serve immediately.

CHEF RACHANA

NEPAL

IT ONLY TAKES A FEW MINUTES IN THE EAT OFFBEAT KITCHEN TO KNOW who is running the show. That would be Rachana Rimal, or as the chefs lovingly call her, "Mami." One minute, she stops at a table to taste a sauce, making sure the spices are right. The next, she swoops in to pull someone's ingredients out of the deep fryers at exactly the right moment. Rachana operates as if on a higher plane of consciousness. The easy explanation for this lies with her being the first Eat Offbeat chef—she's been around the longest and knows every recipe. But there is a much longer answer, and that one begins way back in Nepal.

Rachana was born into a well-off, traditional Brahmin family. She lived much of her childhood surrounded by her extended family, about forty-five people in total, which is quite common in many Nepalese and Hindu households. There was the grandfather who had worked as an administrator for the king and had thirteen children. Brahmin sons often live with their parents after marriage, staying until the father passes away. The daughters-in-law quickly take their places helping to run the household or, if there is help, accompanying the matriarch during her day.

Rachana's own mother, Padma, would be awake by four o'clock in the morning to begin the process of preparing meals, taking her spot in the kitchen rotation and remaining there throughout the day. The daily care of her children fell to the older unmarried girls of the household— in Padma's case, Rachana's two older sisters. If their father wasn't overseeing their family farm, two days away in the Terai Valley, he would be around after dinner, which was at seven o'clock every day, to watch over the younger children and put them to bed. Rachana doesn't even know what time her mother went to bed, just that she was always awake and always busy.

"LIKE MY MOTHER ALWAYS SAYS, 'FOOD IS GOD.' ALL NEPALESE SAY THAT, NOT ONLY MY MOM. ANYTHING THAT GROWS FROM THE GROUND IS GOD-GIVEN. SO HOW MUCH YOU SERVE, GOD WILL GIVE THAT MUCH TO YOUR FAMILY. SERVING IS OUR CULTURE."

Of course, this all seemed normal to Rachana. Children don't know enough of the world yet to judge whether their family operates like other families. They assume that everyone lives like they do, and young Rachana was no different. She considered herself lucky to have constant companions and playmates. When she was around age thirteen, her immediate family moved into their own house. It was then that Rachana really began learning to cook from her mom. "That's why I have the passion, the cooking passion," she says. "I love to cook because of all the time I was with Mom. . . . Whatever skill she had, I took it from her."

When Rachana and her sisters were older, each wanted to inherit the special fryer used for making *sel roti,* a sweet, ring-shaped treat made with rice flour, the Nepalese answer to doughnuts. To make up her mind, Padma decided to hold a contest. Each daughter had to make her own sel roti, and the best one would win the fryer. Rachana soaked her jasmine rice overnight, strained it, ground it by hand with a mortar and pestle, and pushed the grains through cheesecloth so only the finest flour remained. She added sugar to the finely ground flour and fried it in ghee. She won, of course, and still loves to make fresh sel roti coated in sugar.

In her mid-teens, Rachana married her husband, Sunil Rimal. After the ceremony, she moved in with the Rimals, a smaller household consisting of her husband, her mother-in-law, and her grandmother-in-law. That was it.

A big surprise was their daily menu. The family was a touch more modern, serving foods that were a bit spicier than what her own family enjoyed. Now she laughs when she recalls those days. "I couldn't eat too much because it's so hot, oh my God, what is this food, I don't like!" She also had to learn how to make momos, the South Asian dumplings that have come to represent Nepalese food the world over. She turned to the kitchen helper of the household, a member of another Hindu social class, who taught her to use a little bit of fatty and creamy ingredients in the momo filling to get it nice and juicy. At the time, most Nepalese made momos with buffalo meat or chicken, but Rachana, an off-and-on vegetarian, had to learn and devise new filling recipes for herself. And so she raised her family, a son and two daughters, in Kathmandu, never needing to work, but usually busy in the kitchen.

This is the knowledge that Rachana brought with her when she moved to New York City in 2006. Nepal's government had been unstable for a decade, and since she could emigrate, she did. (Her husband and two daughters would join her later.) But when she arrived in New York, Rachana realized that she had no real work experience—at least not working in an office. An employment officer instead placed her in a home, as a nanny, where she could do what she does best: mother and nurture. She happily recounts this period of her life, explaining that even now, the child that she cared for "is like my granddaughter, she is not even one point less than my daughter."

And then she met Manal, who was in the beginning stages of creating Eat Offbeat. The nanny job was beginning to wind down, and Rachana was looking for work in a kitchen. She knew she could cook great Nepalese and Indian dishes, but her American repertoire was limited to her beloved mashed potatoes. When Manal offered her the job, she "was the happiest person that day!"

Just like her mother, Rachana thrives when she's busy and the wheels are whirring in her head. This is why she knows when things need to be done in the kitchen and why, even though she spends all week cooking, she manages to find time to teach classes with the League of Kitchens—a business that organizes cooking classes taught by women from around the world. Rachana opens her home to complete strangers to teach them dishes she loves, including her prized sel roti.

CHEF DIAA ✳ SYRIA

FATTOUSH

*Fresh lettuce, tomato, cucumber, and onion
in lemon and olive oil with crispy pita*

SERVES 6 AS A SIDE SALAD

In the Levantine region of the Middle East, there's an entire genre of dishes known as *fattat* that use stale flatbreads as inspiration for a variety of recipes. Fattoush is one of those dishes. The salad comes together with typical summer vegetables, but instead of croutons, fried or baked pieces of pita give the final dish the beloved crunchy texture. Although the instructions here are for baked pita chips, Diaa typically fries the pita when he makes fattoush. If desired, you can fry your own in a neutral-flavored oil over medium-high heat until golden brown, just a minute or two per side, blotting the crispy pita with a paper towel to remove any excess oil.

2 white pitas	4 plum or ⅓ cup cherry tomatoes	¼ cup distilled white vinegar
Olive oil, for brushing the pitas	6 ounces sliced or whole black olives, drained	¼ cup pomegranate molasses (see page xviii)
½ large head romaine lettuce	1 teaspoon kosher salt	2 tablespoons fresh lemon juice
1½ large cucumbers	1 tablespoon ground sumac (see page xix)	½ cup extra virgin olive oil
½ red onion, peeled		

1 Preheat the oven to 375°F. Line a rimmed sheet pan with parchment paper.

2 Brush both sides of the pitas with olive oil and cut them into squares or long triangles. Place the pita pieces on the prepared sheet pan and bake them until they are crisp and golden, 15 to 20 minutes, turning the pieces after 10 minutes for even baking. Set them aside to cool.

3 Trim and thinly slice the lettuce and place it in a large mixing bowl. Slice (or dice) the cucumbers and onion, then toss them in with the lettuce. Seed and dice the plum tomatoes or halve the cherry tomatoes, and add them to the mixing bowl. Stir in the olives and salt.

4 Place the sumac, vinegar, pomegranate molasses, lemon juice, and olive oil in a small mixing bowl and whisk to combine. Pour the vinaigrette over the salad and stir to coat thoroughly. Serve the salad topped with the pita chips.

HEARTS OF PALM SALAD

Hearts of palm and avocado in a simple vinaigrette

Hearts of palm are an oft-overlooked but very nutritious vegetable that can be found in cans in the Latin food aisle. They are actually buds harvested from young palm trees. The flavor is very subtle, almost like artichoke hearts, with a very creamy texture, which lends itself well to this traditional South American salad made with avocados. In the can, hearts of palm come as small stalks or precut, so you may be able to skip a step here if you choose.

2 cups hearts of palm, drained

2 plum tomatoes, seeded and diced

2 slightly firm avocados

3 tablespoons extra virgin olive oil

2 tablespoons distilled white vinegar or fresh lime juice

1 teaspoon kosher salt

1½ teaspoons freshly ground black pepper

1 tablespoon finely chopped fresh cilantro leaves, for garnish

1 Slice the hearts of palm into ½-inch pieces if not precut. Place them in a small mixing bowl and add the tomatoes.

2 Carefully spoon out the insides of the avocados, discarding the pits. Dice the avocado flesh and add it to the bowl.

3 Combine the olive oil, vinegar or lime juice, salt, and pepper in a small mixing bowl and whisk together to form a vinaigrette. Pour the vinaigrette over the salad and fold in gently until the vegetables are thoroughly coated. Serve immediately, garnished with the cilantro.

KATAHAR SALAD

*Shredded jackfruit with fresh tomato and cucumber
in lemon-cilantro dressing*

SERVES 4 AS A SIDE SALAD

Because of its versatility as a meat substitute, jackfruit is increasingly available in American grocery stores (see page xvii). But before it became popular among the health-conscious, it was a staple of many South and Southeast Asian cuisines. For this dish, look for jackfruit canned in brine as opposed to sugary syrup.

2 cans (20 ounces each) jackfruit in brine, drained

4 tablespoons olive oil

½ cup finely chopped yellow onion

1 small garlic clove, peeled and minced

Pinch of fenugreek seeds (see page xvii)

Pinch of ground turmeric

Pinch of ground cumin

1 cup coarsely chopped plum tomatoes

1 cup coarsely chopped cucumber

2 tablespoons fresh lemon juice

1 cup cilantro leaves, chopped

1   Fill a medium pot with water to a depth of 4 inches and bring to a boil over medium-high heat. Add the jackfruit and cook, covered, until fork-tender, about 30 minutes. Drain and chop the jackfruit into 1-inch pieces. (It should look shredded.)

2   Place 3 tablespoons of the olive oil in a large skillet over medium-high heat. Line a plate with paper towels. Once the oil is hot, add the jackfruit pieces and pan-fry until they are golden brown and crunchy, about 15 minutes. Place the finished jackfruit on the towel-lined plate using a slotted spoon.

3   Add the remaining 1 tablespoon of olive oil to the same pan, and lower the heat to medium. Once the oil is hot, add the onion and garlic and sauté for about 2 minutes, then add the fenugreek seeds, turmeric, and cumin. Continue to sauté until the onion is tender, about 3 minutes more. Remove the pan from the heat.

4   Combine the jackfruit and onions in a medium serving bowl. Add the tomatoes, cucumber, lemon juice, and cilantro and stir to combine. Serve immediately.

CHEF DHUHA ✳ IRAQ

TABBOULEH SALAD

Mint-scented parsley salad with fresh tomato, onion,
and bulgur in lemon–olive oil dressing

◁ SERVES 6 TO 8 AS A SIDE SALAD ▷

Tabbouleh is a perfect side dish for everything from kibbeh to chicken and rice. In some countries (Lebanon, Syria, Palestine), parsley is the main attraction, but in Western culture, the salad has seen a role reversal, with bulgur taking center stage. Dhuha's Iraqi version is somewhere in between—the bulgur and parsley balance each other out.

Every family with an heirloom tabbouleh recipe makes it differently, based on personal preference (such as by omitting the onion). Some variations add a little bit of pomegranate molasses or bitter orange—a sharper type of the citrus, native to Asia and Africa, that has been cultivated in many corners of the globe. If you opt to try these variations, reduce the lemon juice accordingly.

½ cup fine bulgur

3 cups finely chopped fresh flat-leaf parsley leaves

3 cups finely chopped fresh mint leaves

1 cup diced, seeded plum tomatoes or halved cherry tomatoes

1 cup finely chopped scallions

½ cup fresh lemon juice

½ cup extra virgin olive oil

1 tablespoon ground sumac (see page xix)

1 tablespoon kosher salt

1 Place the bulgur in a bowl and cover it by ½ inch with room-temperature water. Let it soak until all the liquid is absorbed, 10 to 15 minutes.

2 Combine the parsley, mint, tomatoes, and scallions in a medium mixing bowl. Stir gently until the vegetables are thoroughly mixed.

3 Whisk the lemon juice, olive oil, ground sumac, and salt in a small bowl until emulsified, about 2 minutes.

4 Pour the dressing over the vegetables and stir gently to coat thoroughly.

5 Gently stir in the bulgur. Serve immediately.

CHEF RACHANA ✳ NEPAL

— LENTIL SOUP —

Warming black lentil soup
in jimbu-flavored spicy broth

< SERVES 4 AS A MAIN DISH >

An easy and healthful weeknight meal, this lentil soup gets its Nepali flavor from *jimbu*, a wild allium found in the Himalayas, along with fresh ginger, garlic, garam masala, and asafetida. Black lentils are also known as *urad dhal*, and sometimes come packaged split or skinned. You want the whole version here.

3 tablespoons ghee

1 yellow onion, peeled and finely chopped

1 tablespoon freshly grated ginger

2 garlic cloves, peeled and finely chopped

1 bird's-eye chile, finely chopped (see page xvii)

1 tablespoon cumin seeds

1 cup diced plum tomatoes

1 tablespoon garlic powder

1 tablespoon onion powder

1 tablespoon ground cumin

1 tablespoon garam masala

1 tablespoon jimbu (see page xviii)

1 tablespoon ground turmeric

1 pinch asafetida powder (see page xvi)

1 cup black lentils

1   Melt the ghee in a large pot over medium heat. Once it is shimmering, add the onion, ginger, garlic, chile, and cumin seeds to the pot and sauté until the onion and chile are tender, about 5 minutes.

2   Lower the heat slightly and slowly stir in the diced tomato, garlic powder, onion powder, ground cumin, garam masala, jimbu, turmeric, and asafetida powder. Cook, stirring, until the spices are fragrant, about 5 minutes.

3   Add the lentils and 4 cups of water. Raise the heat to medium and bring the water to a boil. Once it is boiling, reduce the heat to a simmer and cook, covered, until the lentils are tender, about 40 minutes. Serve immediately.

CHEF LARISSA

CENTRAL AFRICAN REPUBLIC

TOWARD THE END OF 2017, A FEW MEMBERS OF THE EAT OFFBEAT TEAM attended an event for the local PBS station. The night's theme was female empowerment. When she was prompted to answer the question "Who inspires you?" Larissa Lakouetene didn't have to think twice. She even wrote her answer on a placard, made sure to get a photograph of herself holding the sign in front of the camera, and sent the picture to the women whose names she wrote on the placard: her mother and grandmother back home in Bangui, the capital of the Central African Republic.

It was Larissa's grandmother, Josephine, who helped raise her while her mother worked full-time as a pediatric nurse. Larissa and her seven siblings often helped out in the fields outside the city. When they got home, the girls helped Josephine cook for the family, picking up her traditional recipes in the process.

"EAT OFFBEAT IS MY FAMILY NOW."

But her mother and grandmother taught Larissa and her sisters more than just recipes; they passed on a legacy of strength. As an only child, Josephine had to marry young and could not depend on her family to assist in raising her two children. She'd pick up any work she could while her husband, Larissa's grandfather, was serving as a soldier. And Josephine's courage wasn't limited to the hearth. At one point, during an insurrection, with rebels committing atrocities in villages nearby, Larissa's brother pleaded with their grandmother to leave Bangui with them. She defiantly refused, stating that she wasn't afraid. He literally had to carry her out of her village in order to get her to safety. It is that fortitude that was passed down to Larissa's mother, and then to Larissa.

Most importantly, both women made sure that Larissa and her siblings received enough education to succeed anywhere. After they wed, Larissa and her husband, Tony, moved to Burkina Faso for graduate school before heading back to Bangui. As they started their own family, Larissa established a career in banking while Tony worked for the United Nations.

It was thinking about her grandmother and mother's resilience that inspired Larissa through the dark moments after leaving the Central African Republic. With her five children, including a newborn, in tow, she left her husband back home and made her way through West Africa to New York City. Her husband eventually joined them, and the family was united again. In New York, Larissa would bring her newborn, Grace, with her to English classes despite her teacher's concerns. "I had to learn English. It's the first language here! And I couldn't leave my child," she explains. When the International Rescue Committee (IRC) asked if she'd like to work for Eat Offbeat, she thought about how her mother had gone back to work once her father left. She knew she too had to provide for her family.

Once a week, Larissa speaks to her family back home, catching up on news and stories of how her grandmother hasn't lost her fighting spirit. Eat Offbeat has even hired her oldest daughter, Benicya, to help with deliveries when she's not in school. Larissa's daughters have a strong bond with fellow Eat Offbeat employee and Central African native Rose (see page 95). For Larissa, coming to work helps give her a sense of community. Back home, she frequently stopped by to visit her mother and grandmother, but now, it's her friends from work that she visits. According to Larissa, "Eat Offbeat is my family now."

RED PEPPER SOUP

Pureed red bell peppers with brioche croutons

⟨ SERVES 6 TO 8 AS A STARTER ⟩

The Central African Republic has various regional dishes, including *fufu* made from cassava, *foutou* made from plantains, chicken stews, freshwater fish and seafood, and yams, which are indigenous to the nation. This soup from Larissa—which was created in collaboration with Chef Juan—is easy to pull together and delicious with fresh croutons. Be prepared for the evaporated milk to curdle when it's heating, but don't worry—it'll come back together while pureeing in Step 5.

1 brioche loaf	3 cups finely chopped yellow onions	Cilantro sprigs, for garnish
3 tablespoons olive oil	1 tablespoon ground red pepper	Extra virgin olive oil, for garnish
5 cups finely chopped red bell peppers	4 cups chicken stock	Flaky sea salt and freshly ground black pepper, for garnish
	1 cup evaporated milk	

1 Preheat the oven to 400°F. Line a sheet pan with parchment paper.

2 Cut the brioche loaf into 1-inch cubes and place them on the prepared sheet pan. Bake until they are brown and crunchy, about 5 minutes. Be careful not to burn the croutons. Set aside to cool.

3 Heat the olive oil in a large pot over medium heat. Once the oil is hot, add the bell peppers and onions and sauté until the peppers are tender and the onions are golden, about 10 minutes.

4 Stir in the ground red pepper and chicken stock. Bring to a boil, then lower the heat to a simmer, cover the pot, and cook until the peppers and onions are very soft, about 30 minutes. Stir in the evaporated milk and simmer for 10 minutes more. Remove the pot from the heat.

5 Carefully pour the soup into a blender and puree until smooth, about 30 seconds. Serve the soup topped with croutons and garnished with cilantro sprigs, a drizzle of olive oil, and a sprinkle of salt and pepper.

— MA'AREENA SOUP —

Spaghetti and tomato soup with ground beef and mozzarella

◄ SERVES 4 TO 6 AS A MAIN DISH ►

Y ou might associate spaghetti and similar noodles with Italy, but the Middle East also has a history of using thin wheat noodles in its cuisine. This includes a popular lentil and angel hair dish served during iftar, the evening meal breaking the fast of Ramadan. Diaa also makes Ma'areena Soup, which may seem reminiscent of Italian Bolognese but tastes distinctly Syrian with the seven spices blend.

1 pound dried spaghetti

1 tablespoon olive oil

1 pound ground beef (80% lean)

1⅓ cups finely chopped yellow onions

2 plum tomatoes, minced

2 tablespoons tomato paste

1 teaspoon freshly ground white pepper

1 teaspoon freshly ground black pepper

½ teaspoon kosher salt

1 teaspoon seven spices (see page xix)

8 ounces mozzarella cheese, shredded

1 cup fresh flat-leaf parsley leaves, minced

Flat-leaf parsley sprigs, for garnish

1   Break the spaghetti into 2½- to 3-inch lengths. Set aside.

2   Heat the olive oil in a large pot over medium heat. Once the oil is hot, add the ground beef and onions. Stir the beef and onions together and cook until the onions are tender and the meat is starting to brown, about 10 minutes.

3   Stir the tomatoes and tomato paste into the beef and onions. Cook, stirring frequently, 5 minutes more.

4   Slowly stir in the white and black pepper, salt, and seven spices. Add 4 cups of water and allow everything to come to a slow boil, about 10 minutes.

5   Stir in the spaghetti and cook until it's al dente, 5 to 7 minutes. Remove the pot from the heat.

6   Stir in the shredded cheese, letting it melt in with the spaghetti. Add the minced parsley, stir to distribute it slightly, and serve immediately, garnished with parsley sprigs.

GRAIN
DISHES

ALGERIAN COUSCOUS

Traditional semolina couscous
with chicken, beef, and vegetables

— 68 —

SHANTHI'S COUSCOUS

Vegetarian couscous
with curry leaves and cilantro

— 73 —

VEGETARIAN BIRYANI

Cinnamon-scented rice
with vermicelli, potato, sweet peas,
carrots, and raisins

— 75 —

JOLLOF RICE

Traditional West African rice dish

— 79 —

RIZ GRAS

Guinean rice with chicken,
cabbage, and carrots

— 82 —

MUJADDARA

Syrian lentils with bulgur
and caramelized onions

— 84 —

ADAS POLOW

Iranian rice
with lentils and raisins

— 86 —

ROOZ

Basmati rice
with crispy potatoes,
chickpeas, and tuna

— 87 —

RED RICE

Tomato-infused basmati rice
with fried onions,
raisins, and almonds

— 90 —

OUZÉ

Festive Lebanese rice
with beef and chestnuts

— 92 —

MINATA'S OKRA

Okra rice
with chicken thighs

— 98 —

ALGERIAN COUSCOUS

Traditional semolina couscous with chicken, beef, and vegetables

◅ SERVES 4 TO 6 AS A MAIN DISH ▻

C ouscous is a cornerstone of Algeria's cuisine, wherever you live—in the country or the diaspora. Nowadays, most Algerians use dried, packaged couscous, as opposed to couscous made by hand. They prefer to steam it rather than soaking it to keep the couscous fluffy. At the store, pick fine-grain or "Moroccan" couscous, called *m'hamsa* in North Africa, not the larger pearl couscous. Any vegetables you have on hand, provided they're not too watery, can be used and cooked together in Step 3.

Traditionally, this dish might be served with the veggies and meat piled on top, but those at the table would know to mix it all together on their plates. If you want to prepare this in a *couscoussier* (a traditional steamer made of two pots), prepare the stew in the base and steam the couscous three times in the steamer basket (omit the cheesecloth), adding 1 to 2 cups of water and breaking up any clumps between each session.

2 medium white onions, peeled

3 tablespoons vegetable oil

1 pound stew beef, cut into 1-inch cubes

1 pound skinless, boneless chicken thighs, cut into 1-inch cubes

2 plum tomatoes, quartered

4 teaspoons kosher salt

1 teaspoon freshly ground black pepper

1 cup (8 ounces) canned chickpeas, drained

1 cup diced carrot

2 scallions, finely chopped

2 cups cubed eggplant (½-inch cubes)

1 cup diced zucchini

16 ounces frozen peas, defrosted, or about 2 cups fresh

4 cups fine-grain couscous, rinsed and drained

2 tablespoons unsalted butter

1 Grate the onions (using the large holes of a box grater or the grating disk of a food processor). Place the grated onion in a strainer set over a bowl and press to extract juice. Reserve the juice and solids separately.

2 Heat 2 tablespoons of the vegetable oil in a large pot over medium heat. Once the oil is hot, add the onion solids and sauté until they are golden, about 10 minutes. Add the beef and chicken and cook until the meat begins to brown, 8 to 10 minutes more. Cover the meat with 5 cups of water, then add the tomatoes, salt, and pepper to the pot. Bring to a simmer and cook the stew, covered, for 45 minutes.

3 Add the chickpeas, carrot, scallions, eggplant, zucchini, and peas to the stew and simmer until vegetables are cooked through, 15 to 20 minutes more.

4 Pour the couscous into a small mixing bowl and stir in the remaining 1 tablespoon of oil. Add 1 cup of water (or enough to coat the couscous) and mix everything together with your hands. Let sit until the liquid is absorbed, stirring occasionally with a fork or your hands to prevent clumping, 5 to 10 minutes.

5 Meanwhile, bring a medium pot of water to a simmer over low heat. Line a colander with a layer of cheesecloth.

6 Place the soaked couscous in the lined colander and set it over the simmering water, making sure that the bottom of the colander does not touch the liquid. (If steam escapes from a space between the colander and the pot, wrap a kitchen towel around it.) Steam, uncovered, for about 15 minutes. (Begin timing the moment you see steam rising through the couscous.)

7 Transfer the couscous to a mixing bowl (reserve the lined colander). Add the butter and let it melt, then slowly stir in 1 cup of stock from the stew, adding it $\frac{1}{4}$ cup at a time so the couscous absorbs it. Add the reserved onion juice. Fluff the couscous with a fork, then let it rest for 5 minutes.

8 Return the couscous to the lined colander, replace the kitchen towel if using, and continue steaming until the couscous is light and fluffy and cooked al dente, another 15 minutes.

9 Remove the colander from the pot and spoon the couscous into a shallow serving bowl. Pour the remaining stock over the top. Place the meat and vegetables on top and serve immediately.

CHEF EL BAHIA

ALGERIA

WHEN EL BAHIA FANGHORE GREW UP IN ALGERIA, MANY OLD-SCHOOL traditions were still part of everyday life. One of those traditions was the recurring *twiza*. A twiza is an occasion when a group of people come together to achieve a common goal, such as harvests or the food preparation in advance of a wedding. These gatherings are something she looks back on fondly when discussing her hometown, Mila.

Food and cooking always played a big part of El Bahia's life in Algeria. As one of seven children, and one of the eldest, it fell to her to help her mother, Rahima, prepare daily meals. And they truly were daily. Eating out wasn't a normal part of Algerian life. The family never went to restaurants or ate out for more than a snack. Even in New York, El Bahia doesn't truly partake in the enormous restaurant scene. That amount of cooking meant that almost every recipe was tweaked and perfected, and the pressure for each meal to be tasty never lifted.

"WE HAVE THIS RELATIONSHIP THAT IS BEYOND WORK AND BEYOND PROFESSION. . . . WE FEEL LIKE A FAMILY."

Couscous is so essential to Algerian food culture that it is often considered the national dish. Up until the 2000s, El Bahia, her mother, and various members of her family would regularly congregate for a days-long twiza during summer months in order to prepare food for winter storage. A lot of times, those twizas involved making couscous by hand. The process is labor intensive. To start, semolina flour is slowly mixed together with water. When enough tiny granules form, everything is sifted to ensure uniformity, and then laid out in the sun to dry. The finished couscous is then stored in a dry place. The process would go on until the women felt they had enough couscous in reserve; often hundreds of pounds would be needed to get a family through the winter, especially if they always had Friday meals centered on couscous.

Rahima, though, would still make small batches at home. The smell of fresh couscous steaming instantly inspires nostalgia for El Bahia. "In my childhood, I loved the smell of couscous. I still have it in my nose because my mom had a

stock for everyday use, so she prepared it every day from scratch. It is fresh and it is amazing." She admits to having smuggled in a small amount of good Algerian couscous (store-bought, not handmade) when she immigrated to New York toward the end of 2016, and she refills her stash of "special" couscous whenever she visits home.

Though she's an immigrant and not a refugee, El Bahia came to Eat Offbeat through an IRC training program. After she prepared a test meal of cauliflower and cheese (not a traditional Algerian dish—one she invented because she likes cheese) for Manal, Wissam, and the team, she quickly became an integral part of the delivery team. She truly enjoys her time in and out of the kitchen with her Eat Offbeat friends. "We have this relationship that is beyond work and beyond profession. . . . We feel like a family." She's also amazed by life in New York. With her family so far away now, life here has given her an opportunity for personal growth. "I feel the difference between even the person that I was and the person that I am now and the person I hope to become one day."

SHANTHI'S COUSCOUS

Vegetarian couscous with curry leaves and cilantro

⟨ SERVES 4 TO 6 AS A SIDE DISH ⟩

Shanthi's version of couscous is a unique take on the grain dish. The turmeric, green beans, and curry leaves give the Mediterranean dish a wonderful South Asian twist.

1 teaspoon kosher salt

1 teaspoon ground turmeric

10 ounces fine-grain couscous

3 tablespoons olive oil

1 cup diced bell pepper

1 cup diced eggplant

1 cup diced carrot

1 cup diced potato

1½ cups chopped green beans

1 cup yellow onion, chopped

5 curry leaves (see page xvii), finely chopped

½ cup roughly chopped fresh cilantro leaves, for garnish

1 Place 2 cups of water in a large saucepan over high heat and bring it to a boil. Carefully stir in the salt and turmeric and boil for 1 minute. Add the couscous, bring it back to a boil, then cover the saucepan, remove the pot from the heat, and let the couscous sit until the water is fully absorbed, about 10 minutes.

2 Heat 2 tablespoons of the olive oil in a large nonstick skillet over medium-high heat. Once the oil is hot, add the bell pepper, eggplant, carrot, potato, and green beans, stirring to coat, and cook, stirring occasionally, until the vegetables have started to brown, about 15 minutes. Stir the cooked vegetables into the couscous and set it aside, covered.

3 Place the remaining 1 tablespoon of olive oil in the skillet and set it over medium heat. Once the oil is hot, add the onion and curry leaves and cook, stirring frequently, until the onion begins to brown, 8 to 10 minutes. Add the mixture to the couscous and stir to combine.

4 Serve immediately, garnished with the chopped cilantro.

─ VEGETARIAN BIRYANI ─

Cinnamon-scented rice with vermicelli, potato,
sweet peas, carrots, and raisins

⊰ SERVES 4 TO 6 AS A MAIN DISH ⊱

This mixed rice dish may be popularly associated with Indian cuisine, but *biryani*—or *biriyani* or *birani*, as it is known in different parts of the world—is also prevalent throughout Middle Eastern regions with large Muslim populations. Dhuha's version adds wheat vermicelli noodles, fried potatoes, and raisins. She usually makes it with a lot of beef, but this adaptation was made for Eat Offbeat's vegetarian customers. If you can't find wheat vermicelli, look for *fideos*—short, dried noodles that are traditionally toasted and used in Spanish cooking—or capellini.

2 tablespoons canola oil

1 cup wheat vermicelli noodles

1 cup fresh or frozen peas

1 cup diced carrot

1 cup peeled and diced russet potato

¼ cup black or golden raisins (or a combination)

1 cup basmati rice

1 cinnamon stick

¼ teaspoon ground turmeric

2 teaspoons kosher salt

1 tablespoon seven spices (see page xix) or biryani spices (see Note)

½ teaspoon ground cardamom

1 teaspoon ground cinnamon

1 Heat 1 tablespoon of the oil in a small saucepan over medium-high heat. Once the oil is hot, add the vermicelli and toast until the noodles are golden, about 2 minutes. Carefully add ½ cup of water to the pot, cover it, and bring the water to a boil. Reduce the heat to low and simmer until the noodles are tender and the water is absorbed, about 10 minutes. Remove the pot from the heat and set it aside.

2 Heat the remaining 1 tablespoon of oil in a large nonstick skillet over high heat. Once the oil is hot, add the peas, carrot, and potato and pan-fry until they are tender and starting to brown, about 10 minutes. Stir in the raisins and cook until they plump and begin to brown, about 2 minutes more. Remove the pan from the heat and set it aside.

RECIPE CONTINUES

3 Bring 1½ cups of water and the rice, cinnamon stick, turmeric, and salt to a boil in a large pot over high heat. Once the water is boiling, cover the pot, reduce the heat to low, and simmer until the rice is cooked, 10 to 15 minutes.

4 Whisk together the seven spices, cardamom, and ground cinnamon in a small bowl.

5 Add the vermicelli to the rice, then gently stir in the spices, making sure to evenly incorporate them and coat the grains. Stir in the vegetables and raisins. Serve immediately.

NOTE Dhuha buys a brand of biryani spices called Abido Spices from Middle Eastern grocery stores.

CHEF DIAA ❋ SYRIA
VERMICELLI RICE
Toasted wheat noodles with rice

◄ **SERVES 4 TO 6 AS A SIDE DISH** ►

Rice mixed with vermicelli is a traditional side dish in the Middle East. The vermicelli adds a bit of flavor and a splash of color to plain white rice.

1 tablespoon canola oil	1 cup basmati rice, rinsed	Freshly ground black pepper
½ cup broken vermicelli noodles	1 teaspoon salt, plus more as needed	

1 Heat the oil in a small saucepan over medium heat. Once the oil is hot, add the vermicelli. Stir the noodles while they toast until they are golden, about 3 minutes. Remove from the heat. Transfer to a plate and set aside.

2 Bring 1½ cups of water and the rice and salt to a boil in a medium pot over high heat. Once the water is boiling, cover the pot, turn the heat to low, and simmer until the rice is cooked and the water is absorbed, 10 to 15 minutes.

3 Add the vermicelli to the rice, then gently stir in additional salt and pepper to taste. Serve immediately.

JOLLOF: A HISTORY

Jollof rice (see page 79) is an indispensable element of West African cuisine. This single-pot rice dish is reddened by tomato paste and typically accompanied by meat or smoked or fresh fish. Traditional seasonings and spices include curry powder, garlic, chili powder, bay leaves, Scotch bonnet peppers, dried thyme, and cloves.

The invention of jollof rice can be traced back to the medieval Wolof Empire, which ruled Senegalese and Gambian regions from the 1200s to the 1600s. One of its kingdoms, Jolof, lends its name to the iconic rice dish. However, this term is not used by the Senegalese; rather, the dish is referred to as *thiéboudienne* or *ceebu jen* when the protein is fish, and *thiebou yapp* or *ceebu yapp* when it is beef. In Gambia—and some Senegalese regions— it is called *benachin*, which translates to "one pot."

Jollof rice is integral to the culinary realms of Nigeria and Ghana. As is common when multiple regions lay claim to the same foods, there is ceaseless debate over which country produces the best jollof dishes. Nigerians prefer to use parboiled long-grain rice, whereas Ghanaians favor basmati rice that is cooked with meat stock and tomatoes. Nigerian jollof is spiced with bay leaves, and Ghanaians further emphasize the dish's heat with *shito*, an oily relish that combines hot peppers, ginger, onion, and shrimp. Of course, there are varied cultural assumptions about the most "authentic" versions of jollof; Nigerians often reject the inclusion of bell peppers, carrots, and cabbage, while Ghanaians feel similarly toward leafy greens.

— JOLLOF RICE —

Traditional West African rice dish

⟨ **SERVES 6 TO 8 AS A SIDE DISH** ⟩

Few dishes are as popular in West Africa as jollof rice. Every family has its own recipe, each region has its own variation, and everyone thinks theirs is the best. At the very least, every version includes rice, tomatoes, and tomato paste. Edafe learned this version from his mother, who insisted that he perfect the dish before leaving for college. If you can't find the reddish Cameroon black pepper, substitute your favorite subtle ground chile, whether it's Kashmiri or cayenne.

5 tablespoons olive oil

1 cup jasmine rice

2 tablespoons tomato paste

2 cups vegetable stock

1 cup finely diced yellow onion, plus 1 cup thinly sliced

1 cup finely chopped yellow bell pepper

1 cup finely chopped red bell pepper

1 cup finely chopped green bell pepper

1½ cups diced tomatoes

1 teaspoon curry powder

1 teaspoon Cameroon black pepper powder (see page xvii)

1 tablespoon dried thyme

Kosher salt, to taste

1 Heat 3 tablespoons of the olive oil in a large pot over medium heat. Once the oil is hot, stir in the rice, tomato paste, and vegetable stock. Lower the heat to a simmer, cover the pot, and cook the rice until it is tender, about 15 minutes. Remove the pot from the heat and set it aside, still covered.

2 Heat 1 tablespoon of the olive oil in a large nonstick skillet over medium-high heat. Once the oil is hot, add the diced onion and the yellow, red, and green bell peppers and sauté until the onion is golden, 8 to 10 minutes. Stir in the tomatoes, curry powder, Cameroon black pepper powder, and dried thyme. Cook for 5 minutes more, lowering the heat if spices start to burn.

3 Heat the remaining 1 tablespoon of olive oil in a small skillet over medium-high heat. Add the sliced onion and fry until crispy and dark golden brown, about 10 minutes.

4 Add the vegetables to the rice and top with the crispy onion. Add salt to taste and serve immediately.

CHEF EDAFE

NIGERIA

AS ONE OF THE EARLY EMPLOYEES OF EAT OFFBEAT, EDAFE OKPORO helped establish the friendly tone found in the kitchen—his warm personality and jovial nature instantly put everyone at ease. When he comes back to visit, the Nigerian native is overwhelmed with hugs.

Though he no longer runs operations in the Eat Offbeat kitchen, Edafe keeps himself busy. He is a podcast host, author, social media maven, and, among other things, executive director of the RDJ Refugee Center for homeless refugees in New York, but his story starts in Warri, a large oil hub city in the Niger Delta. There, Edafe and his three siblings grew up under the watchful eye of their mother. She was primarily a housewife but acquired a reputation for her excellent cooking. At one point in their childhood, she owned a small restaurant that did well.

Since Edafe was the youngest child, he didn't need to help out in the kitchen as much, so it wasn't until he was leaving for college—the first in his family to go— that Edafe began learning the family's traditional dishes. Of those, he mastered only one: jollof rice.

His mother needed to know that he would be able to take care of himself and have some taste of home. So he learned by helping her make it, remembering all the details that make her jollof rice better than everyone else's. And finally, when he felt ready, he made it for her. He'd go on to make the dish every Sunday night while studying for his bachelor's degree—it became a hit with his roommates.

Later on, Edafe began working as an HIV counselor and advocate for the LGBTQ community in Nigeria. During this time, he picked up a few other recipes, but he always kept jollof rice in rotation. Even today, Edafe seeks out smoky Cameroon pepper for just the right touch and keeps the dish rich since he maintains that "West Africans love oily foods." And when he stopped by the kitchen to teach everyone his way of making the rice, that was one of the few things he and one of Eat Offbeat's other Nigerian chefs could agree on.

He looks back on his time at Eat Offbeat with fondness. "It is still in my heart," he says.

CHEF MINATA ✳ GUINEA

— RIZ GRAS —

Guinean rice with chicken, cabbage, and carrots

⊰ **SERVES 6 TO 8 AS A MAIN DISH** ⊱

Cabbage is found in a range of traditional dishes throughout the African conti-nent, including the ever-popular *mafe*, or peanut stew common to West Africa, and this chicken and cabbage rice dish from Minata's home country, Guinea. When small carrots are in season, you can add them whole for extra visual oomph—they'll need an extra 5 minutes to soften in Step 3. Minata's recipes are always flexible and this one is no exception—it can accommodate almost any sturdy vegetable (eggplant is a good option—cut it into 2-inch pieces and add it with the carrots in Step 3), so use whatever you have on hand. The same goes for the type of chicken you use—just adjust the browning and cooking times accordingly.

⅓ cup olive oil

2 pounds skinless, boneless chicken thighs, cut into 1-inch cubes

1 cup finely chopped yellow onion

1 cup diced plum tomatoes

3 garlic cloves, peeled and finely chopped

2 bay leaves

2 tablespoons tomato paste

1 cup finely chopped fresh flat-leaf parsley leves

1½ cups diced russet potatoes

½ cup diced carrot

1 tablespoon freshly ground black pepper

6 cups chopped green cabbage

5 cups chicken stock

1 cup uncooked basmati rice

1 tablespoon kosher salt

1   Heat the olive oil in a stockpot over medium-high heat. Stir in the chicken and cook until it begins to brown, about 15 minutes.

2   Stir the onion, tomatoes, garlic, and bay leaves into the pot. Lower the heat to medium, and cook until the onion has softened and the garlic is fragrant, about 5 minutes.

3   Stir in the tomato paste, parsley, potatoes, carrot, and black pepper. Thoroughly combine, then cook until the carrot has begun to soften, about 5 minutes.

4   Add the cabbage, using tongs to fully incorporate it, if necessary. Pour in the chicken stock and lower the heat to a simmer. Cook, uncovered, until the vegetables are tender, about 30 minutes.

5   Remove the vegetables with tongs (leaving the chicken) and set them aside. Add in the rice and cook until the rice is fluffy, 20 minutes. Add the vegetables back in and heat the mixture through, 3 to 4 minutes. Remove the bay leaves, stir in the salt, and serve.

— MUJADDARA —

Syrian lentils with bulgur and caramelized onions

⊰ SERVES 4 TO 6 AS A SIDE DISH ⊱

Dishes of grains and beans are classic the world over because of their economy, heartiness, and comforting warmth. The addition of browned onions and yogurt sauce elevates the dish beyond its humble origins. Here, the onions are pan-fried, but Diaa prefers to deep-fry them for maximum crunchiness.

¼ cup olive oil

1 cup finely chopped yellow onion, plus 1 cup thinly sliced

¾ cup green lentils

2 teaspoons kosher salt

1½ teaspoons freshly ground black pepper

1 cup extra-coarse bulgur or farro

Vegetable oil, for deep-frying

2¾ cups plain yogurt

2 cups diced cucumber

2 tablespoons dried mint

Chopped fresh mint leaves, for garnish (optional)

1 Heat the olive oil in a large saucepan over medium heat. Once the oil is hot, add the chopped onion and sauté until it begins to brown, about 10 minutes.

2 Add 4 cups of water to the pan, raise the heat to high, and bring to a boil. Stir in the lentils, 1 teaspoon of the salt, and the pepper. Bring back to a boil, reduce the heat to low, and simmer, covered, until the lentils are al dente, about 10 minutes.

3 Add the bulgur, stir everything together, and cook over low heat until the liquid is absorbed and the grains are fully cooked, about 1 hour.

4 Line a plate with paper towels. Pour the vegetable oil into a heavy-bottomed saucepan to a depth of at least 2 inches and clip a candy thermometer to the side, making sure it doesn't touch the bottom. Heat the oil over medium-high heat to 375°F. Deep-fry the sliced onion until golden brown, 2 to 3 minutes, and transfer to the towel-lined plate to drain.

5 Stir together the yogurt, cucumber, dried mint, and the remaining 1 teaspoon of salt in a medium bowl.

6 Place the bulgur mixture in a serving dish and top with the fried onions. Serve with the yogurt sauce on the side, topped with fresh mint, if desired.

— ADAS POLOW —

Iranian rice with lentils and raisins

Green lentils add a healthful component to this traditional Persian side dish. Be careful when cooking the raisins as they can start burning after they plump.

1 cup green lentils, rinsed and drained

1 cup basmati rice

2 teaspoons unsalted butter

1 teaspoon kosher salt

2 tablespoons vegetable oil

1 cup finely chopped yellow onion

1½ teaspoons ground turmeric

½ cup black raisins

1   Place the lentils and 1 cup of water in a large pot over high heat. Bring to a boil, then lower the heat to a simmer, cover, and cook the lentils until they're soft, about 20 minutes.

2   Stir the rice into the pot and add 1½ cups of water and the butter. Cover and simmer until the water is fully absorbed, 8 to 10 minutes. Stir in the salt, remove the pot from the heat, and set aside.

3   Heat 1 tablespoon of the vegetable oil in a small nonstick skillet over medium-high heat. Once the oil is hot, add the onion and sauté until golden, about 8 minutes. Add the turmeric and stir until the onion is fully coated. Scoop the onion out of the pan to a small bowl and set aside.

4   Remove the pan from the heat and add the remaining 1 tablespoon of oil. Once the oil is warmed from the residual heat, place the pan back on the stove over medium heat. Add the raisins and cook until they begin to plump, about 2 minutes. Remove the pan from the heat.

5   To serve, layer the onions over the rice and lentil mixture in a serving dish, before topping with the raisins.

— ROOZ —

Basmati rice with crispy potatoes, chickpeas, and tuna

⟨ SERVES 6 TO 8 AS A SIDE DISH ⟩

The hardest part of this dish—but also the best part—is the final flip. You'll want to showcase the crispy bottom layer of potatoes, something everyone will want to get a part of. For the tuna, splurge on a can of high-quality fish.

1 cup basmati rice

¼ cup fresh cilantro leaves

⅓ cup fresh dill fronds

1 large russet potato

4 tablespoons vegetable oil

¾ cup finely chopped yellow onion

1 teaspoon ground turmeric

2 garlic cloves, peeled and minced

1½ tablespoons dried fenugreek leaves (see page xvii)

1 can (5 ounces) good-quality tuna in oil, drained

1 teaspoon freshly ground black pepper

1 teaspoon ground cumin

1 teaspoon kosher salt

3 tablespoons fresh lemon juice

1 can (15 ounces) chickpeas, drained

¼ cup sesame seeds

1   Place the rice in a large pot and cover with 2 cups of water. Let it sit for 2 hours. Then place the pot over medium-high heat and bring the water to a boil. Lower the heat to a simmer, cover the pot, and cook until the rice is tender, about 15 minutes. Set the pot aside, still covered.

2   Meanwhile finely chop the cilantro and dill. Peel the potato and slice into ¼-inch-thick disks.

3   Heat 2 tablespoons of the vegetable oil in a large nonstick skillet over medium-high heat. When the oil is hot, add the onion and sauté until it is caramelized, 8 to 10 minutes.

4   Stir the turmeric into the onion. Once the onion is thoroughly coated, stir in the chopped cilantro and dill. Remove the pan from the heat.

5   Add the garlic, dried fenugreek, and tuna, breaking the tuna up as you stir. Add the pepper, cumin, and salt. Stir in the lemon juice, then fold in the chickpeas.

RECIPE CONTINUES

6 Heat the remaining 2 tablespoons of oil in a large pot over high heat. When the oil is hot, sprinkle in the sesame seeds, creating an even layer on the bottom of the pot. Then carefully layer the potato slices on top of the seeds, removing the pot from the heat if the oil begins to splatter. Let the sesame seeds and potato slices crisp slightly, about 1 minute.

7 Add the rice and the tuna-chickpea mixture to the pot in alternating layers. Reduce the heat to low, cover, and cook until the mixture is warmed through, about 10 minutes more.

8 Remove the pot from the heat and let it rest for 5 minutes. Remove the cover and place a platter on top of the pot. Using your hand to hold the platter in place, carefully flip the pot and platter over. Gently lift the pot and the rice will begin falling out. The golden sesame-crusted potatoes will crown the rice. Serve immediately.

QUEST FOR THE GOLDEN CRUST

The perfect crispy bottom to Nasrin's rooz is hard to master, as it is with another Persian dish, *tahdig*. Tahdig, whose name means "bottom of the pot" in Farsi, is made by frying the bottom layer of rice in a pot, while the rice on top of it steams and cooks. And while getting the right ratio of crispy rice to fluffy rice is important, so is the final flip, which, when done correctly, leaves the golden layer centered on your platter.

CHEF DHUHA ✳ IRAQ

— RED RICE —

Tomato-infused basmati rice with fried onions, raisins, and almonds

‹ SERVES 6 TO 8 AS A SIDE DISH ›

The red in this dish's name comes from the tomato paste, which adds an earthy flavor to the rice. The sweet raisins and crunchy almonds add to the uniqueness. Seven spices is a seasoning blend, usually with a black pepper and allspice base.

¾ cup raw almonds

3 medium yellow onions, peeled and thinly sliced

2 teaspoons kosher salt

¾ cup vegetable oil

2 cups basmati rice

3 tablespoons tomato paste

1 vegetable bouillon cube

½ cup golden raisins

1½ teaspoons ground cardamom

1½ teaspoons seven spices (see page xix)

1 Place the almonds and 3 cups of water in a medium pot over medium heat. Boil until the almonds are softened, about 30 minutes. Drain and skin them, then rinse and set them aside.

2 Place the onions in a medium mixing bowl, add 1 teaspoon of the salt, and stir to coat. Set them aside.

3 Place ¼ cup of the vegetable oil and the rice, tomato paste, and bouillon cube in a large pot over high heat. Toast the rice, stirring, for 1 minute, being careful not to let it burn, then add 4 cups of water and the remaining 1 teaspoon of salt. Once the mixture comes to a boil, lower the heat to a simmer, cover, and cook until the rice is fluffy and the water is fully absorbed, about 30 minutes.

4 While the rice is cooking, heat the remaining ½ cup of the oil in a medium nonstick skillet over high heat. Once the oil is hot, add the onions and sauté until they are golden brown, about 20 minutes. Transfer them with a slotted spoon to a bowl. Then add the almonds to the skillet and sauté until they are toasted and brown, 2 to 3 minutes. Remove them with a slotted spoon and add them to the onions. Then add the raisins to the skillet and pan-fry until they are plump, 4 to 5 minutes; set them aside with the onions and almonds.

5 Stir the cardamom and seven spices into the cooked rice. Add the onions, almonds, and raisins and stir. Serve immediately.

OUZÉ

Festive Lebanese rice with beef and chestnuts

⟨ SERVES 4 TO 6 AS A MAIN DISH ⟩

When Manal and Wissam's mother visits them in the States, Wissam always requests her *Ouzé*. This Lebanese dish can be made with slow-braised lamb, but their mother's version uses beef. This dish is delicious with jarred, no-sugar-added chestnuts, but try it with freshly roasted chestnuts when they're in season.

Their mother's trick to giving the rice a nice brown color is to pan-fry two tablespoons of sugar in two teaspoons of hot oil until it's toasted, adding one tablespoon to the broth in Step 2, and the other tablespoon with the rice in Step 6.

⅔ cup vegetable oil

2 pounds stew beef, cut into 1-inch cubes

½ cup sliced carrot

1 medium yellow onion, peeled

½ cup red cooking wine

2 teaspoons kosher salt

2 teaspoons freshly ground black pepper

1 bay leaf

1 cinnamon stick

1 cup black or golden raisins (or a combination)

¼ cup pine nuts

½ cup shelled pistachio nuts

½ cup whole raw almonds

1½ pounds ground beef (80% lean)

1 teaspoon ground cinnamon

½ teaspoon ground nutmeg

2 cups long grain rice

10 to 12 jarred or roasted chestnuts, quartered

1 Heat 3 tablespoons of the oil in a large heavy-bottomed stockpot or Dutch oven over medium-high heat. Once the oil is hot, add the stew beef, carrot, and whole onion, stirring to coat with oil. Cook until the onion is tender and the beef is beginning to brown, about 15 minutes. Remove and discard the onion.

2 Lower the heat to medium and add the cooking wine, 1 teaspoon of the salt, and 1 teaspoon of the pepper. Cook, covered, until any browned bits are loosened, about 5 minutes. Add 8 cups of water, the bay leaf, and cinnamon stick. Bring to a boil, reduce the heat to low, and simmer, covered, until the meat becomes tender, about 1 hour.

3 Meanwhile, place the raisins in a small mixing bowl and cover them with warm water. Let them soak until they begin rehydrating, about 30 minutes. Once they are plump, drain them and set them aside.

4 Use a slotted spoon to remove the beef from the pot and set it aside. Remove the pot from the heat and set it aside to reserve the cooking liquid.

5 Line a large plate with paper towels. Heat the remaining oil in a large saucepan over medium-high heat. Add the pine nuts and pistachios and toast until the nuts have turned golden, about 1 minute. Using a slotted spoon, remove the nuts and drain them on the lined plate. Quickly add the almonds and toast until they turn golden brown, about 2 minutes. Remove them to the lined plate to drain. Reserve the oil.

6 Add the ground beef to the oil in the saucepan, place over medium-high heat, and cook, stirring occasionally, until the beef has browned, about 10 minutes. Stir in the plumped raisins, cinnamon, nutmeg, and the remaining 1 teaspoon each of the salt and pepper. Add 4½ cups of the cooking liquid from Step 4 and bring it to a boil. Stir in the rice, bring it back to a boil, reduce the heat to medium-low, and simmer, uncovered, until the rice has absorbed the liquid, about 10 minutes. Remove the pan from the heat.

7 Scoop the rice onto a platter and garnish with the beef, fried nuts, and chestnuts. Serve immediately with ¾ cup of the reserved cooking liquid as a sauce, if desired.

HEIRLOOM RECIPES

Ouzé has always had a special place in Manal and Wissam's family—it's their mother's signature dish for Sundays and holidays, and she learned the dish from their grandmother. It was almost a given that this would be their mother's contribution to potluck gatherings with other family members, at the homes of various aunts or uncles. To this day, it remains the dish that reminds Wissam the most of family gatherings.

Wissam has always loved the amazing flavor and crunchiness that the fried nuts bring to the dish, so he always makes sure to save some separately for the leftovers that will be plentiful the following couple of days. And if he runs out, he fries some extra when reheating the leftovers.

CHEF ROSE

CENTRAL AFRICAN REPUBLIC

IT'S EASY TO GET ROSE NZAPA AYEKE TO CRACK A SMILE. THOUGH SHE carries the wise aura of someone who went through unbelievable hardships back in the Central African Republic, her face instantly lights up at talk of her only surviving daughter, and when she's speaking about childhood memories of her grandparents. Her mother grew up in a village in the northeastern part of the country, close to Chad, Sudan, and what is now South Sudan. She left for the capital, Bangui, ultimately marrying Rose's father and becoming a flight attendant, but she often brought her children back home.

Village life gave Rose a different perspective than her days in Bangui. Her grandparents farmed cotton and lived without electricity, meaning they relied on traditional open fire cooking. She remembers her grandmother using shea butter, peanut oil, and cotton oil when cooking, as well as eating the traditional staples of corn and millet. Even though they were "always cooking" for that day's meals, there were a few items they could make ahead of time. Her grandfather would mix ground peanuts and seasoning with corn, sometimes adding in ground beef or other nuts if available, before enveloping everything in a leaf packet. This dumpling-like meal would keep for a week or two and was very convenient when unexpected guests stopped by.

HER FACE INSTANTLY LIGHTS UP AT TALK OF HER ONLY SURVIVING DAUGHTER, AND WHEN SHE'S SPEAKING ABOUT CHILDHOOD MEMORIES OF HER GRANDPARENTS.

In Bangui, life was more modern. Rose's family had an oven and other electric appliances. Meals would be accompanied by a cup of coffee or a glass of wine. Instead of corn and millet, cassava flour was more prevalent, she recalls. Today, with the increase of food brought in by United Nations relief efforts, plantains have become popular, an ingredient she didn't remember having growing up. Rose continued learning how to cook from her mother, and she often learned from mistakes. "She always says to me, 'No, don't touch this, undo this!'" A favorite meal her mother made was the intensive but rewarding dish of beignets with black-eyed peas.

During the 2002 armed rebellion and coup attempt, Rose escaped Bangui with her surviving daughter, fleeing to Cameroon. At first, she attempted to reunite with a sister who had long ago settled in Germany but instead accepted an offer to come to the United States. Another sister relocated to Australia. Despite the distance, the sisters continue to be close with one another, each learning different things about their new homes and sharing the information. Luckily, they are still able to visit family in the Central African Republic.

When she arrived in the United States in 2007, Rose worked in commercial kitchens and as a home attendant before landing at Eat Offbeat, where she came aboard as an effusive delivery woman and unofficial ambassador (the member of the company most likely to be requested or thanked by name for a delivery). In New York, Rose is passing down her culture to her daughter, Ata-Kadija, a prospective medical student. She is confident that their shared love of food from their homeland fortifies the already strong bond between them. Whenever Rose is sad, it is Ata-Kadija who makes her laugh, lifting her spirits. Rose has even taught her how to make *koko*, the typical meat and greens dish eaten with *fufu*, an essential starchy food made of boiled yams.

A DAY IN THE KITCHEN

7:00 AM: Chefs arrive. Hugs and morning chatter ensue.

7:30 AM: One of the chefs works on reorganizing storage areas and unpacking all the new ingredients received overnight. The others prepare the work stations, and ingredients start flowing out of the walk-in fridge and onto the stations. By this time, the chefs have looked at the production board to see what orders are going out today and what dishes they are in charge of.

8:30 AM: The smell of Eat Offbeat's signature cardamom-scented Nescafé and milk permeates the kitchen. The chefs alternate between making coffee and tea for the morning ritual. Today, Bashir is making coffee. Tomorrow, Shanthi will be concocting a special milk tea to wake everyone up.

9:00 AM: Diaa is standing over an industrial-size food processor, filling it with chickpeas and eyeballing the tahini ratio for his hummus. Bashir peers over the vat of frying oil, waiting for a batch of kibbeh to bob to the surface. Minata carefully folds samosa dough, pinching it over the filling and arranging it in a perfect line on the sheet pan. The synchronized choreography of the kitchen is not met with silence, however—lively chatter floats over the day's playlist, which is a Nasrin special today.

10:00 AM: Delivery team members start arriving. Nasrin makes sure they get some coffee.

11:00 AM: The push for the lunch catering hour has peaked. Everyone is focused, there's no room for distractions. The music is replaced by the loud noises of a hectic kitchen. Chefs and delivery team members run around, making sure all orders get packaged and dispatched on time: Sarujen calls out for the samosas he still needs for a delivery. Rose hurries to cut up some pita bread to go with the hummus platter she just packed. Bashir runs over to the oven to check if Mariama's Chicken Yassa is ready to go.

1:00 PM: All lunch deliveries for the day have gone out. Shanthi sets up for family meal: She dishes up some leftover rice, a new okra dish that Minata is testing out, a shrimp curry that Mariama prepared, and a salad. Bashir texts the team in the upstairs office to come down for lunch.

2:00 PM: Chefs are testing new ideas in the kitchen—Nasrin has made a loaf of magically fluffy bread, coated with sesame seeds and tinged with a touch of sweetness.

—MINATA'S OKRA—

Okra rice with chicken thighs

⤖ **SERVES 4 TO 6 AS A MAIN DISH** ⤗

Americans may think of okra as a vegetable of the American South, where it shows up in gumbo or is quickly fried for a summer appetizer. But this sun-loving plant comes from somewhere in southern Asia, Arabia, or east Africa (its origin is still being researched). Regardless, it has long been a popular staple crop in Africa, which is how it made its way to the Americas and the Caribbean.

---

3 tablespoons olive oil

1 pound skinless, boneless chicken thighs, cut into 1-inch cubes

5 small yellow onions, peeled and finely chopped (about 4 cups)

2 plum tomatoes, diced

2 cups chicken stock

1 tablespoon cornstarch (optional)

10 whole okra, sliced into ½-inch rounds (reserve any liquid they release)

1 cup white rice, rinsed

---

1 Heat 2 tablespoons of the olive oil in a medium saucepan over medium-high heat. When the oil is hot, stir in the chicken cubes. Cook the chicken, stirring frequently, until it begins to brown, about 15 minutes.

2 Lower the heat to medium. Stir in the onions and tomatoes. Cook until the onions are soft, about 10 minutes more.

3 Add the chicken stock. Raise the heat to high and bring to a boil, then lower to a simmer. Partially cover and cook until the liquid has reduced, 5 to 10 minutes.

4 If you prefer a thicker sauce, whisk the cornstarch with 3 tablespoons of water in a separate bowl until you have a slurry. Remove the pan from the heat and quickly whisk the slurry into the sauce. Bring to a boil over high heat and boil, stirring, for 1 minute.

5 Meanwhile, prepare the okra rice: Place the remaining 1 tablespoon of olive oil in a small nonstick skillet over medium-high heat. When the oil is hot, slide the okra with their liquid into the pan and cook until it begins to brown, about 5 minutes. Remove from the heat.

6 Pour the rice into a medium saucepan and stir in the okra slices. Add 2 cups of water and place over medium-high heat. Bring to a boil, then lower the heat to a simmer. Cover and cook until the water is absorbed, about 10 minutes. Remove from the heat.

7 To serve, place a few scoops of rice in each bowl, then ladle the saucy chicken over the top.

VEGETARIAN DISHES

SHANTHI'S DHAL

*Split lentils with curry leaf
and coconut milk*

— 102 —

KOWA VARRAI

Coconut cabbage

— 104 —

BONJI CARROT CURRY

*Green beans and carrots
in coconut milk*

— 106 —

TOOR DHAL

Yellow lentil dhal

— 110 —

URAD DHAL

Spicy black lentil dhal

— 111 —

ADAS

*Lentils pureed
with berbere spices*

— 112 —

MANCHURIAN CAULIFLOWER

*Battered and fried cauliflower
in sweet chili sauce*

— 115 —

PANEER AND PEAS

*Vegetarian curry
with paneer cheese*

— 118 —

PANEER CURRY

*Paneer curry thickened
with spices and melon seeds*

— 122 —

KATARICA CURRY

*Fried eggplant
in creamy curry leaf, fenugreek,
and tomato sauce*

— 124 —

NEPALI PIZZA

Rachana's take on flatbread

— 127 —

BHINDI

Okra and potato curry

— 129 —

MITSLAL'S DOLMAS

*Vegetables stuffed
with herbed tomato rice*

— 130 —

— SHANTHI'S DHAL —

Split lentils with curry leaf and coconut milk

◁ SERVES 4 TO 6 AS A SIDE DISH ▷

The food of Sri Lanka isn't as famous as that of other South Asian cuisines. But this curry dhal is a good beginner's lesson. Curry leaves and coconut are cornerstones, as is turmeric and, of course, dhal, whose name in Hindi refers to both lentils and dishes made with them. If you can't find split lentils, try yellow lentils, which will keep their shape. Dhal is traditionally served with a number of sides, such as dosas (opposite page) and *Kowa Varrai* (page 104), coconut cabbage. This version can be served with a steaming side of basmati rice to temper any of the spicy qualities of the curry leaves.

1¼ cups split lentils, rinsed and drained

4 curry leaves (see page xvii)

1 tablespoon ground turmeric

1 tablespoon kosher salt

1 tablespoon vegetable oil

1 cup finely chopped yellow onion

1 cup full-fat coconut milk

1 red bell pepper, chopped, for garnish (optional)

Cooked basmati rice or dosas, for serving

1 Place the lentils, 2½ cups of water, 2 of the curry leaves, the turmeric, and salt in a large pot. Bring to a fast simmer over medium heat, then reduce the heat to low, cover the pot, and cook until the lentils are tender, about 25 minutes.

2 Heat the vegetable oil in a small nonstick skillet over medium-high heat. Once the oil is hot, add the onion and the remaining 2 curry leaves and sauté until golden, 8 to 10 minutes. Remove the skillet from the heat and remove the curry leaves.

3 Stir the coconut milk into the lentils. Spoon the onions over the lentils and garnish with the chopped red pepper, if desired. Serve immediately over basmati rice.

DOSAS
Crepe-like pancakes

Dosas are thin, crunchy pancakes that originated in southern India and Sri Lanka. The batter is supposed to ferment until foamy—if your kitchen is on the cool side, you might need to let it ferment a little bit longer than overnight. Serve alongside Shanthi's Dhal (opposite page), or turn to Rachana's Samosas for a great potato filling (page 16).

1 cup skinned and split black lentils (urad dhal), rinsed and drained

1 cup cooked basmati rice

1½ cups all-purpose flour

2 medium white onions, peeled and chopped

1½ teaspoons mustard seeds

½ teaspoon fennel seeds

6 curry leaves

½ cup canola oil, plus more for cooking the dosas

1 teaspoon ground turmeric

1 tablespoon kosher salt

1 Place the lentils in a medium mixing bowl and add water to cover by at least 2 inches. Let sit until the lentils are bigger in size, 2 to 3 hours. Drain.

2 Pour the lentils into a blender, add the rice and 1 cup of water, and puree.

3 Transfer the puree back to the mixing bowl and stir in the flour and 2 cups of water until well combined. Cover the batter and let ferment at room temperature until it's foamy and smells a bit sour, 6 to 8 hours (or longer as needed).

4 Heat ½ cup of the canola oil in a small saucepan over medium heat. Add the onions, mustard seeds, fennel seeds, and curry leaves, and cook until the onions are tender and brown, 10 to 15 minutes. Discard the curry leaves. Add the onion mixture to the fermented batter along with the turmeric and salt and stir gently to combine. The batter should be runny—add water if it is not.

5 Heat 1 tablespoon of the canola oil in a large nonstick skillet over medium heat. Once the skillet is very hot, quickly scoop out ½ cup of batter and pour it into the skillet in a spiral. Smooth out the batter as thinly as possible. Cook the dosa until the bottom is golden brown (tiny bubbles may from on the surface), about 5 minutes. Flip and cook the other side to set, about 1 minute. Remove the dosa from the pan. Repeat with the remaining batter. Serve immediately.

—KOWA VARRAI—

Coconut cabbage

> ◁ **SERVES 4 TO 6 AS A SIDE DISH** ▷

Coconut plays a big part in Sri Lankan cuisine—so much so that locals call it "the tree of life." Not only is it readily available, but it's also a versatile ingredient, lending itself to dishes in solid and liquid form. Here it amplifies a cabbage dish that can be served alongside spice-laden curries. Even though Shanthi and her son Sarujen will attest that coconuts found in New York are nothing like those found in Sri Lanka, this side dish is refreshing all the same. Serve it along with curries, plain rice, or dhal.

2 tablespoons canola oil

1 cup diced yellow onion

1½ pounds green cabbage, cored and sliced

½ teaspoon fennel seeds

5 curry leaves, sliced (see page xvii)

½ cup unsweetened coconut flakes

1 teaspoon chili powder

Kosher salt

1 teaspoon fresh lemon juice

Chopped fresh flat-leaf parsley leaves, for garnish

1 Place the oil in a large nonstick skillet over medium-high heat. When the oil is hot, add the onion and cook until translucent, 5 to 7 minutes.

2 Add the cabbage, fennel seeds, and curry leaves to the skillet, stirring, and cook until the cabbage is no longer green and becomes tender, about 10 minutes.

3 Add the coconut flakes and chili powder and stir to combine. Cook until the coconut softens slightly and the chili powder is fragrant, a few minutes more. Add salt to taste, then add the lemon juice and remove the pan from the heat.

4 Garnish with the chopped parsley and serve.

BONJI CARROT CURRY

Green beans and carrots in coconut milk

SERVES 4 TO 6 AS A SIDE DISH

This simple green bean curry with carrots and coconut is a wonderful accompaniment to dhal or on its own over rice. Sri Lankans typically cut the green beans into ¼-inch pieces on the diagonal, but you can also cut them into ½-inch pieces.

¼ cup vegetable oil

2 cups sliced yellow onion

1 bird's-eye chile, thinly sliced (see page xvii)

1 cup sliced carrot (about ½-inch thick)

1 pound green beans, sliced

3 cups sliced plum tomatoes

½ teaspoon kosher salt

5 garlic cloves, peeled and minced

1½ teaspoons ground turmeric

4 curry leaves, thinly sliced (see page xvii)

1 cup full-fat coconut milk

1 Place 2 tablespoons of the oil in a large nonstick pan over medium heat. Once the oil is hot, add the onions and chile and cook, stirring occasionally, until the onions are tender and begin to brown, about 10 minutes.

2 Pour the remaining 2 tablespoons of oil into the pan. Add the carrot and green beans, stirring to incorporate, and cook, stirring occasionally, until the carrot and green beans soften and begin to brown, about 20 minutes.

3 Stir in the tomatoes and salt, and cover the pan. Cook until the tomatoes have softened, about 5 minutes.

4 Stir in the garlic, turmeric, curry leaves, and 1 cup of water. Re-cover the pan and cook until the carrot is very tender, about 10 minutes. Stir in the coconut milk, lower the heat, and simmer until the curry has thickened slightly, about 5 minutes. Remove the pan from the heat and serve.

CHEF SHANTHINI

SRI LANKA

THOUGH SHANTHINI SIVAKUMAR CAME TO WORK FOR EAT OFFBEAT IN LATE 2017, she is no stranger to the commercial kitchens of New York City. In fact, the Jaffna, Sri Lanka, native worked with Eat Offbeat chefs Jean-Baptiste Meda and Mitslal (page 114) prior to joining the team. Though more than 20 million people live in the New York metropolitan area, the immigrant and refugee communities are tight-knit. This has led more than a few Eat Offbeat employees to get to know one another prior to being hired. The irony with Shanthi (as she is known in the kitchen) is that, unlike most of the Eat Offbeat staff, she didn't truly step into her own kitchen until she was married.

Shortly after her wedding, she moved with her husband to Lebanon to join his brother who was working there. Her brother-in-law started cooking for the entire household. Shanthi got inspired by the dishes he made, and she gradually learned from him. Judging by the quality of the food she prepares today, he must have been an amazing teacher and she an exceptional student!

Sri Lankan cuisine relies heavily on rice, coconut, and fresh produce. It is that last element that Shanthi remembers fondly: the sweet-and-sourness of fresh mangosteens and rambutans, plus the huge, juicy mangoes native to Jaffna that put North American mangoes to shame.

She also misses one thing in particular: Sri Lankan curry powder. It's not unusual for a household to make their own curry mix for everyday use, with the dry-roasted spices, but without turmeric (which distinguishes it from the Indian curry powder more familiar to Western cooks).

Shanthi started at Eat Offbeat helping in the kitchen. Of course, it wasn't long before the team discovered how amazing her dishes were and started featuring them on the menu. Her continuously happy mood and smile bring joy to the team in the most stressful situations. She also often cooks the daily lunches for the team, reminding everyone to take a short break and eat before they run out of energy. And she's brought in her real family to join her Eat Offbeat family—her son Sarujen, who is studying film and television at LaGuardia Community College, successfully manages and schedules the deliveries.

TOOR DHAL

Yellow lentil dhal

⟨ SERVES 4 TO 6 AS A SIDE DISH ⟩

The yellow lentils in this dish make it a little bit sunnier than other dhals. Yellow lentils, also known as *toor dhal* or *arhar dhal*, are mild and nutty and are often found split and skinned. This is a milder but heartier version of dhal than the ones found in Sri Lanka. If you cannot find yellow lentils, substitute yellow split peas.

1 cup yellow lentils, rinsed and drained

1 tablespoon ground turmeric

2 bay leaves

1 cinnamon stick

¼ teaspoon ground nutmeg

1 tablespoon kosher salt

1 tablespoon ghee

1 tablespoon cumin seeds

1 tablespoon jimbu (see page xviii)

1 cup chopped yellow onion

¼ teaspoon asafetida powder (see page xvi)

1 teaspoon garam masala

1 teaspoon chili powder

½ cup diced plum tomato

1 tablespoon, plus 1 teaspoon, chopped fresh ginger

½ cup chopped fresh cilantro leaves

5 garlic cloves, peeled and chopped

1   Place the lentils and 4 cups of water in a large pot over medium heat. Add the turmeric, bay leaves, cinnamon stick, nutmeg, and salt. Cover, bring to a simmer, then reduce the heat to low. Cook until the lentils are soft, about 35 minutes. Remove the pot from the heat and set it aside, still covered.

2   Melt the ghee in a medium skillet over medium heat, then add the cumin seeds and jimbu. Sauté until toasted and fragrant, about 2 minutes.

3   Add the onion, asafetida, garam masala, and chili powder. Sauté for 1 minute, then add the tomato. Cook until the tomato softens, about 2 minutes more.

4   Add the ginger, cilantro, and garlic. Stir and cook for 1 minute more. Stir into the lentils and serve immediately.

— URAD DHAL —

Spicy black lentil dhal

⟨ SERVES 4 TO 6 AS A SIDE DISH ⟩

D hal, or dal, is common throughout the South Asian subcontinent. The name applies to both the legumes and the dish you turn them into. This one calls for both black (*urad dhal*) and green lentils, cooked with jimbu, cumin seeds, and asafetida for a hearty, healthful meal.

½ cup black lentils, rinsed and drained

½ cup green lentils, rinsed and drained

1 tablespoon kosher salt

1 bay leaf

3 tablespoons finely chopped fresh ginger

1½ tablespoons olive oil

2 bird's-eye chiles, finely chopped (see page xvii)

1 tablespoon jimbu (see page xviii)

¼ teaspoon asafetida powder (see page xvi)

1 tablespoon cumin seeds

1　Place the lentils and 4 cups of water in a large pot over medium heat. Add the salt and the bay leaf. Cover, bring to a simmer, then reduce the heat to low. Cook until the lentils are tender, 35 to 40 minutes.

2　When the lentils are cooked, stir in the ginger. Cook to infuse the lentils with flavor, about 5 minutes, then remove the pot from the heat.

3　Heat the olive oil in a small skillet over medium-high heat. When the oil is hot, add the chiles, jimbu, asafetida, and cumin seeds, and lightly sauté until the seeds begin to toast, about 2 minutes. Add the mixture to the lentils and serve immediately.

— ADAS —

Lentils pureed with berbere spices

⊰ SERVES 4 TO 6 AS A SIDE DISH ⊱

R ed lentils are cooked until extremely tender in this dish from East Africa. Berbere spices are a cornerstone of Egyptian, Eritrean, and Ethiopian cuisine. The spicy blend is readily available in stores or online—Kalustyan's Ethiopian/ Eritrean blend works nicely—but if you find a recipe you prefer, it can easily be made at home. Adas is delicious served with injera bread—a flatbread made of teff flour. It can be found at some grocery stores, specialty markets, and Ethiopian and Eritrean restaurants.

1 cup red lentils, rinsed and drained	2 garlic cloves, peeled and minced	2 tablespoons berbere spices (see page xvi)
1 tablespoon olive oil	1 can (14 ounces) whole peeled tomatoes, crushed by hand	Kosher salt and freshly ground black pepper
1 cup finely chopped yellow onion	1 tablespoon tomato paste	Black sesame seeds, for garnish (optional)

1 Place the lentils and 4 cups of water in a large saucepan over medium heat. Cover, bring to a simmer, then lower the heat to medium-low. Cook until the lentils are al dente, about 20 minutes. Set them aside.

2 Heat the olive oil in a large pot over medium-low heat. When the oil is hot, add the onion and garlic and sauté until the onion has begun to brown, 12 to 15 minutes.

3 Stir in the tomatoes and tomato paste and raise the heat to medium. Cook, stirring frequently, until the sauce begins to simmer, about 10 minutes.

4 Stir in the berbere spices and simmer until the oil separates and the sauce is slightly reduced, about 20 minutes.

5 Stir in the lentils and cook until they are extremely tender, another 30 to 35 minutes. Add salt and pepper to taste and serve immediately, garnished with the sesame seeds, if desired.

CHEF MITSLAL

ERITREA

LOCATED DIRECTLY NORTH OF ETHIOPIA AND SOUTHEAST OF SUDAN, bordering the Red Sea, Eritrea is where scientists found the oldest hominid skeletal remains to date, and it is possible that the earliest modern humans walked through this land on their way out of Africa. Thousands of millennia later, it would be part of the land known as Punt to the ancient Egyptians. But at Eat Offbeat, it is best known as the home of quietly humble Mitslal Tedla.

Mitslal is always observing and learning. While helping her mother cook as a child, she burned herself when something hot came out of the fire. From then on, she was directed to observe from a distance, keeping far away from the fire, even though that meant not helping her mother cook for her eight younger siblings. But watch she did, eventually making dishes for her mother as an adult.

MITSLAL UNDERESTIMATES HERSELF; SHE IS AN EXCELLENT COOK.

After leaving her childhood home in Eritrea's capital, Asmara, Mitslal spent time in Egypt. She lived there for nine years, coincidentally working as a cook for the mother of one of Manal's Columbia professors. During this time, Mitslal helped in the kitchen, picking up Egyptian recipes and techniques from the cooks.

Soon after she landed in the United States, the International Rescue Committee put her in touch with Eat Offbeat, right at the very beginning of the company's existence. At the first cooking tryouts, alongside Rachana, when the two other cooks waxed poetic about their love of food and its connection to their homelands, Mitslal stayed true to herself. When asked why she wanted the job, she responded, "I have to cook to survive. I'm not good. I'm okay. I cook."

Mitslal underestimates herself; she is an excellent cook. She has picked up recipes from Nasrin and Rachana, sometimes utilizing their techniques and flavors when she cooks at home for herself. But Eat Offbeat means more to her than that. Her fellow chefs are all her friends now, each with something to teach her.

MANCHURIAN CAULIFLOWER

*Battered and fried cauliflower
in sweet chili sauce*

⊰ SERVES 4 AS A MAIN DISH ⊱

An Eat Offbeat customer favorite. The chickpea flour in the coating gives the fried cauliflower a light quality and slightly nutty flavor. While widely available as chickpea flour, you can also find it sold as *besan*, garbanzo bean flour, or chana flour. Seek out corn flour for the batter—not corn meal or masa harina.

1 head cauliflower

½ cup chickpea flour

¼ cup cornstarch

¼ cup corn flour

1 teaspoon garlic powder

1 teaspoon onion powder

1 teaspoon garam masala

2 tablespoons Maggi Hot & Sweet Tomato Chilli Sauce (see page xviii)

1 tablespoon distilled white vinegar

1 tablespoon soy sauce

Vegetable oil, for deep-frying

Sliced scallions, for garnish

1 Core the cauliflower and chop it into 2-inch pieces, breaking between the florets when possible.

2 Fill a large pot with water to a depth of 4 inches and bring to a boil over high heat. As the water is heating, prepare an ice bath in a medium mixing bowl and line a large plate with paper towels.

3 When the water comes to a rolling boil, place the cauliflower pieces into the pot and boil until just fork-tender, about 5 minutes. Drain the cauliflower and immediately place in the ice bath until they're cool to the touch, at least 3 minutes. Drain again, place the pieces on the towel-lined plate, and pat dry. Set aside.

RECIPE CONTINUES

4 Place the chickpea flour, cornstarch, corn flour, garlic powder, onion powder, and garam masala in a large mixing bowl and stir to combine. One at a time, whisk in the Maggi sauce, vinegar, soy sauce, and ½ cup of water until all are fully incorporated and the batter is smooth.

5 Place the cauliflower into the batter and carefully fold with a slotted spoon, thoroughly coating all the pieces. Leave the florets in the batter.

6 Pour the oil into a large heavy-bottomed stockpot or Dutch oven to a depth of at least 2 inches and clip a candy thermometer to the side, making sure it doesn't touch the bottom. Heat the oil to 375°F over high heat, then lower the heat to medium to maintain the temperature during frying. While the oil is heating up, line a large plate with paper towels.

7 Using a mesh strainer, place a large scoop of cauliflower pieces into the oil and deep-fry until the cauliflower is golden brown, about 2 minutes. Remove the pieces and place them on the towel-lined plate. Working in batches, fry the remaining cauliflower, letting the oil return to temperature between batches if necessary. Serve immediately, garnished with scallions.

RECIPE DRIFT

The influence of India and China on Nepal is unavoidable because of its location—a small country, slightly larger than Portugal, nestled between the two countries in the Himalayan mountain range. That influence is reflected in the food of the region. "Manchurian" is one such Indo-Chinese dish that is very popular in Nepal. Manchurian is not just a recipe, it's a technique much like tempura—a method of coating and then frying almost any food, especially chicken or cauliflower, in a spiced, saucy batter. When Rachana brought the dish to the Eat Offbeat kitchen, the recipe changed even more. So what makes for an authentic recipe? At Eat Offbeat, it's what the chefs bring to the kitchen from their own experiences and homelands—but it's also the ways in which they adapt to their new customer base in New York and the ingredients that are available to them.

PANEER AND PEAS

Vegetarian curry with paneer cheese

SERVES 4 TO 6 AS A MAIN DISH

This vegetarian curry comes together around delicious paneer cheese. Paneer is one of the simplest cheeses to make at home, but you can also buy it fresh or frozen.

10 ounces paneer cheese (homemade, page 121, or store-bought, see Note, page 120)

4 tablespoons olive oil

6 ounces frozen peas, defrosted

2 bird's-eye chiles, chopped (see page xvii)

1 tablespoon cumin seeds

¼ teaspoon asafetida powder (see page xvi)

2 bay leaves

1 cinnamon stick

4 curry leaves (see page xvii)

1 cup finely chopped yellow onion

1 tablespoon ground turmeric

6 garlic cloves, peeled and finely chopped

4 teaspoons finely chopped fresh ginger

4 tablespoons unsalted butter

1 beefsteak tomato, finely chopped

1 tablespoon chickpea flour

1 tablespoon ground cumin

2 teaspoons garam masala

1 tablespoon ground coriander

1 tablespoon freshly ground black pepper

½ cup plain yogurt

1 tablespoon dried fenugreek leaves (see page xvii)

1 tablespoon ground Kashmiri chile (see page xviii)

2 tablespoons finely chopped fresh mint leaves

Finely chopped scallions, for garnish (optional)

Chopped fresh cilantro leaves, for garnish (optional)

1 Cut the paneer into ½-inch cubes. Heat 3 tablespoons of the olive oil in a medium nonstick skillet over medium-high heat. Once the oil is hot, add the paneer and sauté until golden on all sides, 8 to 10 minutes. Set the paneer aside in a medium mixing bowl.

2 Add the peas to the skillet and sauté until they begin to brown, about 5 minutes. Set them aside in the bowl with the paneer.

RECIPE CONTINUES

3 Sauté the bird's-eye chiles in the same skillet until toasted, about 5 minutes. Remove the skillet from the heat and set it aside.

4 Heat the remaining 1 tablespoon of olive oil in a large pot over medium heat. Once the oil is hot, add the cumin seeds and lightly brown for about 1 minute. Add the asafetida, bay leaves, cinnamon stick, curry leaves, and onion. Stir and sauté until fragrant, 1 minute more.

5 Add the turmeric, garlic, ginger, and butter to the pot. Sauté until the onion is tender and starting to brown, about 10 minutes.

6 Add the tomato and cook for 1 minute more, then stir in the chickpea flour and cook until the tomato starts to soften and the flour is beginning to cook, about 2 minutes.

7 Stir in the ground cumin, garam masala, coriander, black pepper, and 2 cups of water. Raise the heat to high and bring to a rolling boil.

8 Lower the heat to a simmer and mix in the yogurt and dried fenugreek. Once incorporated, fold in the paneer, peas, and ground Kashmiri chile. Remove the pot from the heat and stir in the mint and sautéed chiles. Remove the bay leaves. Let the curry rest until cooled slightly, about 5 minutes.

9 Garnish with scallions and cilantro, if desired, and serve.

NOTE If using frozen store-bought paneer, soak it in hot water for 2 minutes to defrost. Pat it dry before using.

PANEER

Fresh paneer can be hard to find, even in New York City, though it is often available frozen at international markets and specialty grocers, like Kalustyan's. But making it fresh is worth the extra effort. It's one of the easiest cheeses to make at home, taking about an hour from start to finish. And while you might want to use whatever milk you have on hand, look for something that's minimally processed—nothing ultra-pasteurized.

8 cups whole milk
(see headnote)

¼ cup fresh lemon juice

¼ teaspoon kosher salt

1 Line a large colander with cheesecloth and place it in your sink.

2 Place the milk in a stockpot over medium heat and bring it to a simmer, stirring frequently to keep the milk from burning.

3 When the milk becomes foamy, reduce the heat to low and stir in the lemon juice. The milk will begin to separate into curds and whey.

4 Continue stirring until the milk completely separates, about 10 minutes. Remove the curds and whey from the heat and carefully pour them into the colander. The whey should mostly drain out of the colander.

5 Rinse the curds for 2 minutes with cool water to stop the cooking. Then gently squeeze the cheesecloth to remove all of the water and whey. Tie the cheesecloth and suspend it from your kitchen faucet. Let the liquid drain out, about 5 minutes.

6 Transfer the bag of curds to a plate, unwrap the cheesecloth, and sprinkle the curds with the salt. Shape the curds into a rough square, rewrap them in the cheesecloth, and place another plate on top of the bundle, adding a can of beans or a heavy pot to weigh the plate down. Press the curds until completely solid, about 30 minutes.

7 Use the paneer immediately as directed.

— PANEER CURRY —

*Paneer curry thickened
with spices and melon seeds*

< SERVES 4 TO 6 AS A MAIN DISH >

This paneer curry is thickened with ground spices and *char magaz*, a blend made from a mix of seeds, including roasted black watermelon seeds with the outer shell cracked off. They're available at most specialty grocery stores.

4 dried Kashmiri chiles
(see page xviii)

¼ cup char magaz (see page xvii)

10 ounces paneer cheese
(homemade, page 121, or store-
bought, see Note, page 120)

2 bay leaves

6 curry leaves (see page xvii)

2 bird's-eye chiles, diced
(see page xvii)

1 tablespoon dried fenugreek
leaves (see page xvii)

1½ teaspoons ground cinnamon

1 tablespoon ground mace

2 tablespoons olive oil

2 teaspoons cumin seeds

1 teaspoon asafetida powder
 (see page xvi)

3 tablespoons minced fresh
ginger

2 plum tomatoes, diced

1 tablespoon ground turmeric

2 teaspoons freshly ground
black pepper

1 tablespoon ground cumin

2 teaspoons ground coriander

1 tablespoon sugar

1 cup finely chopped fresh
cilantro leaves

1 Grind the Kashmiri chiles into a powder in a spice grinder or food processor. Set aside.

2 Soak the char magaz in ½ cup of water until soft, about 10 minutes. Drain and set aside.

3 Pat the paneer dry. Cut half of it into bite-size cubes; crumble the rest. Set aside in separate batches.

4 Place 1 bay leaf, 3 curry leaves, 1 bird's-eye chile, the dried fenugreek, cinnamon, and mace in a food processor or spice grinder. Pulse until a fine powder, about 30 seconds, then add the soaked char magaz and process for 1 minute. Set aside.

5 Heat the olive oil in a medium pot over medium heat. Add the remaining 1 bay leaf, 3 curry leaves, and 1 bird's-eye chile along with the cumin seeds and asafetida, and sauté until fragrant, 2 to 3 minutes. Add the ginger and tomatoes and stir until thoroughly combined.

6 Add the turmeric, pepper, ground cumin, coriander, sugar, and the spice mixture from Step 4. As the spices absorb liquid, slowly add water to deglaze the pot and keep them from burning.

7 Stir in the Kashmiri chile powder from Step 1. Cook the curry, stirring occasionally, until it is thickened, about 5 minutes.

8 Slowly fold in the cubed paneer and cilantro. Reduce the heat to low and let the curry cook until fully warmed through, about 5 minutes. Remove from the heat.

9 Serve, topping each portion with the crumbled paneer.

BRAIN FOOD

Made from a nutritious blend of seeds found in common fruits and gourds, *char magaz* can be used in a variety of ways. It can be soaked for hours and ground into a paste to thicken sauces; it is used for making *Thandai*, a drink prepared during the Hindu festival of Holi; and it can even show up in Indian sweets and halwa. But probably its most important use is in traditional *achwani*, a sweet dish made for women shortly after they give birth, to rebuild their strength and boost the health of both mama and newborn. Though *magaz* is the name for muskmelon seeds, the meaning of *char magaz* translates roughly to "four brain," indicating the benefits to the consumer's intelligence and focus.

— KATARICA CURRY —

Fried eggplant in creamy curry leaf, fenugreek, and tomato sauce

◁ **SERVES 4 TO 6 AS A MAIN DISH** ▷

This eggplant curry is a crowd favorite at Eat Offbeat. The eggplant slices need to sweat a bit prior to frying, which helps them crisp up better. If you have extra hands in the kitchen, the two aspects of this dish could be made simultaneously. Like most curries, this is best served over fresh basmati rice.

2 medium eggplants (about 2 pounds), cut into 2 x 1-inch planks

2 teaspoons ground turmeric

1 tablespoon, plus 2 pinches, kosher salt

Vegetable oil, for frying

1 tablespoon fenugreek seeds (see page xvii)

1 cup chopped yellow onion

10 curry leaves (see page xvii)

10 garlic cloves, peeled and minced

2 tomatoes, diced

1 teaspoon chili powder

1 tablespoon ground cumin

1 tablespoon tomato paste

1 tablespoon freshly ground black pepper

2 tablespoons sugar

Cooked basmati rice, for serving

¼ cup fresh cilantro leaves, for garnish

1 Sprinkle the eggplant planks with 1 teaspoon of turmeric and 1 tablespoon of salt. Let the planks rest on a paper towel–lined plate for 15 minutes.

2 To fry the eggplant, pour vegetable oil to a depth of at least 2 inches into a large stockpot or Dutch oven and clip a candy thermometer to the side, making sure it doesn't touch the bottom. Heat the oil to 375°F over high heat, then lower the heat to medium to maintain that temperature during frying. While the oil is heating up, line a large plate with paper towels.

3 Working in batches and using a slotted spoon, place the planks in the oil. Fry until all the sides turn golden, gently stirring, 2 to 3 minutes, and then quickly remove them with the slotted spoon. Place on the towel-lined plate. Set aside.

4 Heat the fenugreek seeds in a small dry skillet over medium heat, just until they become fragrant, about 2 minutes. Remove the seeds from the heat and grind in a food processor or spice grinder. Set aside.

5 Heat 2 tablespoons of oil in a large pot over medium-high heat. Once the oil is hot, add the onion and sauté until lightly browned, about 5 minutes. Add the curry leaves and garlic and sauté for 5 minutes. Add the tomatoes and a pinch of salt and cook for 5 minutes. Stir in the chili powder, cumin, and remaining 1 teaspoon of turmeric, then gently fold in the eggplant planks. Stir in 1 cup of water, another pinch of salt, the tomato paste, black pepper, and ground fenugreek seeds, and continue cooking for 5 minutes more.

6 Remove the pan from the heat and stir in the sugar. Serve over rice, garnished with cilantro.

— NEPALI PIZZA —

Rachana's take on flatbread

This is less Neapolitan wood-fired pizza, more flatbread pizza—it's not authentically Nepali, but it *is* authentically Rachana. She is constantly improvising new dishes, and this creation was an instant favorite at the Eat Offbeat kitchen family meals. Make the crust as thin as possible, as you definitely don't want to have a thick, doughy crust. Semolina flour is made from durum wheat, which is coarser and more complex than all-purpose flour. Luckily, it's available at most grocery stores.

1 cup finely ground semolina flour

1 teaspoon kosher salt

1 tablespoon sugar

1 teaspoon garam masala

1 teaspoon ground cumin

1 cup plain yogurt

3 teaspoons olive oil

1 cup diced carrot

1 green bell pepper, diced

1 red bell pepper, diced

1 yellow bell pepper, diced

1 cup diced plum tomatoes or halved cherry tomatoes

⅓ cup Maggi Hot & Sweet Tomato Chilli Sauce (see page xviii)

1 teaspoon dried oregano

1 teaspoon dried basil

1 teaspoon baking soda

2 tablespoons unsalted butter

1 cup grated Parmesan cheese

1½ cups shredded mozzarella cheese

1 tablespoon chopped scallions, for garnish

1 Stir together the semolina, salt, sugar, garam masala, and cumin in a medium mixing bowl. Mix in the yogurt and 1 cup of water. When thoroughly incorporated, let the batter rest to hydrate the semolina, at least 20 minutes but no more than 1 hour.

2 Heat 1 teaspoon of the olive oil in a large skillet over medium-high heat. Once the oil is hot, add the carrot and green, red, and yellow bell peppers and sauté until tender, about 10 minutes. Lower the heat to medium, add the tomatoes, and cook until they are tender, about 5 minutes. Remove from the heat and set aside.

RECIPE CONTINUES

3   Mix the Maggi sauce with the oregano and basil in a small bowl and set aside.

4   When the batter is finished resting, stir in the baking soda.

5   Preheat the oven to 400°F. Line two sheet pans with parchment paper.

6   Heat the remaining 2 teaspoons of olive oil and $\frac{1}{2}$ teaspoon of the butter in a large nonstick skillet over medium-high heat. When the butter is melted, pour $\frac{1}{3}$ to $\frac{1}{2}$ cup of the batter into the pan and spread it as thinly as possible into a 5- to 6-inch circle. Once the sides are cooked and the bottom has started to brown, flip the flatbread using a spatula. Cook for 2 to 3 minutes on each side, then set the flatbread aside on a prepared sheet pan. Repeat with all the batter, melting $\frac{1}{2}$ teaspoon of butter between each batch.

7   Once all the flatbreads are made, begin assembling the pizzas on the sheet pans. Spread a scant tablespoon of the Maggi sauce mixture over the top of each flatbread. Next, sprinkle the Parmesan cheese evenly over the sauce. Finally, top each flatbread with the vegetable mixture and mozzarella cheese.

8   Place the sheet pans in the oven and bake until the cheese is melted and golden, about 10 minutes. Sprinkle with scallions and serve immediately.

BHINDI

Okra and potato curry

◄ SERVES 4 AS A MAIN DISH ►

Okra is known as *bhindi* in Urdu, and it is standard in Pakistani curries. Here, chiles add spice, while the garlic, ginger, and garam masala round out the flavors.

¼ cup canola oil (or other neutral oil), plus more as needed

1½ pounds okra, sliced into ½-inch pieces

2 cups peeled diced russet potatoes

½ cup sliced yellow onion

4 bird's-eye chiles, thinly sliced (see page xvii)

3 tablespoons peeled and minced garlic

¼ cup peeled and finely chopped fresh ginger

3 cups chopped plum tomatoes

1 teaspoon kosher salt

1 tablespoon garam masala

1 cup chopped fresh cilantro leaves, plus whole leaves for garnish

Cooked rice and pitas, for serving

1 Pour ¼ cup of the oil into a large nonstick skillet over medium-high heat. Once the oil is hot, add the okra and sauté until golden brown, about 15 minutes. Using a slotted spoon, remove the okra and set aside.

2 Add the potatoes to the oil in the skillet, adding another tablespoon of oil, if needed, and fry until golden brown, 8 to 10 minutes. Using a slotted spoon, remove the potatoes and set aside with the okra.

3 Lower the heat to medium and add the onion along with another tablespoon of oil, if needed. Cook the onion until tender, about 5 minutes. Add the chiles and cook until they are fragrant, about 1 minute. Stir in the garlic and ginger and sauté until the onion begins to brown, about 5 minutes.

4 Add the tomatoes to the skillet and cook until they begin to tenderize, about 2 minutes. Stir in the salt and garam masala, and cook until the tomatoes are tender, about 5 minutes more.

5 Stir in ⅓ cup of water, the chopped cilantro, and the okra and potatoes. Reduce the heat to low and simmer until the vegetables are tender and warmed through, about 10 minutes.

6 Serve with rice, pitas on the side, and a garnish of cilantro.

— MITSLAL'S DOLMAS —

Vegetables stuffed with herbed tomato rice

◁ **SERVES 4 TO 6 AS A MAIN DISH** ▷

Y ou've probably heard of Greek dolmas, where a meat-and-rice filling is encased in grape leaves. Here you'll be stuffing hollowed-out vegetables. You'll want to make sure the dolmas are snug in the pot and raised off the bottom.

3 cups fresh flat-leaf parsley leaves

2 tablespoons olive oil

1 small white onion, peeled and diced

2 tablespoons tomato paste

3 plum tomatoes, diced

1 cup finely chopped dill fronds

1 cup white rice

4 cups vegetable stock

2 red or green bell peppers

2 baby eggplants

3 beefsteak tomatoes

2 medium red potatoes

1 large white onion, peeled and sliced

1 Finely chop 1 cup of the parsley and set aside.

2 Place the olive oil in a medium saucepan over medium-high heat. When the oil is hot, stir in the diced onion and cook until it has softened, about 5 minutes.

3 Stir in 1 tablespoon of the tomato paste, along with the diced tomato, chopped parsley, and dill. Cook until warmed through, about 1 minute.

4 Stir in the rice. When fully incorporated, add 2 cups of the vegetable stock. Bring to a boil and then reduce the heat to low and simmer, covered, until the stock is absorbed and the rice is cooked, 10 to 12 minutes. Remove the pot from the heat and set aside. Let the filling cool for at least an hour.

5 Meanwhile, cut the tops off the bell peppers, eggplants, beefsteak tomatoes, and potatoes. Using a small paring knife or a spoon, remove the insides of each. Discard the tops and insides.

6 Stuff the hollowed-out vegetables to the brim with the cooled rice filling. Set aside on a platter.

7 Place the onion slices in a layer on the bottom of a Dutch oven or casserole dish and top with the remaining 2 cups of parsley.

8   Stir the remaining 1 tablespoon of tomato paste into the remaining 2 cups of vegetable stock. Pour into the Dutch oven or casserole.

9   Carefully arrange the stuffed vegetables in the Dutch oven on top of the onion and parsley, tops up. Place over medium-low heat. Cover (with heavy-duty aluminum foil if using a casserole dish) and cook until the vegetables soften, about 20 minutes. Remove from the heat, let cool slightly, and serve.

MEAT
DISHES

CHICKEN KARAHI

*Chicken stewed in turmeric,
garlic, and tomato sauce*

— 134 —

FESENJAN

*Slow-stewed chicken with nuts,
pomegranate molasses, and saffron*

— 136 —

CHARI BARI

*Chicken meatballs
in Nepali-spiced cashew sauce*

— 138 —

KANAWA CURRY

*Squid curry with tamarind
and bird's-eye chile*

— 141 —

CHU LA

Ground chicken curry

— 144 —

CARNE MECHADA

*Venezuelan shredded skirt steak
with sliced peppers and onions*

— 146 —

BEEF KEBAB

*Grilled kebab with pomegranate
and roasted tomato sauce*

— 152 —

NARGES KEBAB

Soft-boiled eggs enrobed in spiced beef

— 154 —

CHARI CURRY

*Chicken curry with ginger,
garlic, and garam masala*

— 157 —

MNAZZALEH

*Eggplants stuffed
with beef and pine nuts*

— 158 —

HALLACAS

*Steamed banana leaf tamales
stuffed with pork and beef*

— 164 —

EGYPTIAN MOUSSAKA

*Baked eggplant and ground beef
with béchamel sauce*

— 167 —

CHICKEN CILANTRO

*Mustard-and-lemon–marinated
chicken with cilantro*

— 169 —

CHICKEN SHAWARMA

*Roasted chicken
in shawarma-spiced yogurt sauce*

— 170 —

POULET YASSA

*Marinated roast chicken
with onions and olives*

— 172 —

—CHICKEN KARAHI—

Chicken stewed in turmeric,
garlic, and tomato sauce

⊰ SERVES 4 TO 6 AS A MAIN DISH ⊱

Situated between the Middle East and South Asia, Afghanistan's cuisine is influenced by all of Asia. Here, you may be reminded of India with garam masala and turmeric, but this curry is less intense spice-wise than, say, a curry from Punjab.

3 tablespoons vegetable oil

1½ cups chopped yellow onions

2 tablespoons minced garlic

1 teaspoon kosher salt

1 teaspoon cumin seeds

1 teaspoon ground coriander

1 teaspoon ground turmeric

½ teaspoon garam masala

½ teaspoon freshly ground black pepper

1 pound skinless, boneless chicken thighs, cut into 1-inch cubes

4 teaspoons finely chopped fresh ginger

4 plum tomatoes, quartered

Cooked basmati rice, for serving

Cilantro sprigs, for garnish (optional)

1   Place the vegetable oil in a 4-quart saucepan over medium heat. When the oil is hot, add the onions. Cook, stirring frequently, until the onions are translucent and tender, about 10 minutes.

2   Stir in the garlic and cook until fragrant, about 1 minute. Slowly stir in ½ teaspoon of the salt, the cumin seeds, coriander, turmeric, garam masala, and black pepper. Thoroughly coat the onions and garlic with the spices and cook until fragrant, about 2 minutes.

3   Add the chicken, ginger, and the remaining ½ teaspoon of salt and cook for 15 minutes, stirring frequently.

4   Add the tomatoes and 1 cup of water. Stir and cook until the chicken is cooked through, about 10 minutes. Remove from the heat.

5   Serve with rice, garnished with cilantro, if desired.

FESENJAN

Slow-stewed chicken with nuts,
pomegranate molasses, and saffron

⊰ SERVES 4 TO 6 AS A MAIN DISH ⊱

Fesenjan is one of the first dishes Nasrin ever made, and it remains her favorite. Although it's traditionally made with walnuts, she prefers cashews—but you can use either or a mix of both. This stew is one of the most famous Persian dishes, and it has spread throughout the country from the northern part of Iran, where it originated. Find a great recipe for *tachin* (Persian saffron rice) or *tahdig* (Persian crunchy rice) for serving with the stew.

2 pounds skinless, boneless chicken thighs

A few saffron threads

1 cup boiling water

⅓ cup vegetable oil

3 cups chopped white onions

1 tablespoon ground turmeric

¾ cup cashew flour (see headnote, page 138)

1 tablespoon kosher salt

1 bottle (10 ounces) pomegranate molasses (see page xviii)

⅓ cup sugar

Pomegranate seeds (see box on page 137), for garnish

Cooked basmati rice, for serving

1 Preheat the oven to 350°F. Line a sheet pan with parchment paper.

2 Cut the chicken thighs into quarters and place them on the prepared sheet pan. Bake until fully cooked, about 30 minutes. Lower the oven temperature to 200°F and keep the chicken in the warm oven until Step 9.

3 Steep the saffron in the cup of boiling water. Set aside.

4 Heat the vegetable oil in a large saucepan over medium heat. When the oil is hot, add the onions and sauté until very tender, about 15 minutes. Stir in the turmeric, thoroughly coating the onions. Cook for 2 minutes more.

5 Stir in the ground cashews and cook, stirring frequently and allowing them to brown on the bottom of the pan, about 5 minutes more.

6 Slowly add the saffron water and deglaze the saucepan, scraping up any browned bits that have loosened, about 1 minute. Then stir in the salt.

7 Stir in 2 cups of water and bring it to a rolling boil. Lower the heat so that the liquid simmers and cook until it's reduced, about 30 minutes.

8 Slowly stir in the pomegranate molasses and simmer until it's incorporated into the sauce, about 10 minutes.

9 Add the sugar and cook, stirring to dissolve it, about 15 minutes. Add the chicken pieces. Simmer everything together to reduce the sauce and heat the chicken thoroughly, 10 minutes more. Remove from the heat.

10 Transfer stew to serving bowls, top with pomegranate seeds, and serve with rice on the side.

REMOVING THE JEWELS FROM THE POMEGRANATE

To watch Nasrin open and seed a pomegranate is to watch a master. She uses pomegranate so frequently it has become a joke in the kitchen. But these fruits aren't simple to seed, and peeling them apart often means a big mess. Plus, the tricky thing about pomegranate juice, Nasrin says, is that it doesn't come out of clothes. Her method minimizes spraying and will make sure no rogue seeds shoot off into the kitchen or fall onto your workspace.

First, cut around the crown of the fruit to remove it, like hulling a strawberry. Then slice the pomegranate vertically six ways to create slices. To seed it, hold the slice of fruit in your palm, skin side up, over a bowl, and whack it with a spoon—the seeds will fall into your hand and juice droplets will be minimal. You may need to stop to remove some of the inner spongy layer in between whacks.

— CHARI BARI —

Chicken meatballs in Nepali-spiced cashew sauce

◄ MAKES ABOUT 30 MEATBALLS ►

Throw out any notion of beef-, pork-, or lamb-based meatballs. This chicken dish, which Rachana makes at home by deep-frying the meatballs, is distinctly Nepali in flavor from all of the spices. The tomato-based sauce is more like a curry than marinara, making it perfect for scooping over rice. Cashew flour for the sauce can be found in the baking section of many grocery stores or online.

FOR THE MEATBALLS
½ teaspoon kosher salt

½ teaspoon freshly ground black pepper

½ teaspoon onion powder

½ teaspoon ground cumin

½ teaspoon garlic powder

1½ teaspoons garam masala

¼ teaspoon ground cinnamon

½ teaspoon ground cardamom

1 pound ground chicken

1 large egg, beaten

½ cup dried bread crumbs

FOR THE SAUCE
1 cinnamon stick

1 tablespoon freshly ground black pepper

10 green cardamom pods

2 black cardamom pods

2 tablespoons dried fenugreek leaves (see page xvii)

1 star anise pod

2 tablespoons coriander seeds

2 tablespoons cumin seeds

2 tablespoons ghee

2 cups chopped yellow onions

1 tablespoon onion powder

1 tablespoon ground cardamom

1 tablespoon garam masala

1 can (14.5 ounces) whole peeled tomatoes, pureed in a blender

2 tablespoons tomato paste

3 cups chicken stock

1 cup cashew flour

¼ cup cornstarch

Fresh cilantro leaves, for garnish

Chopped scallions, for garnish

Pinch of flaky Himalayan salt, for garnish

1 Preheat the oven to 400°F. Line a sheet pan with parchment paper.

2 Make the meatballs: Combine the salt, black pepper, onion powder, ground cumin, garlic powder, garam masala, ground cinnamon, and ground cardamom in a medium mixing bowl. Add the ground chicken, egg, and bread crumbs and mix together using your hands.

3 Form the chicken mixture into 1-inch meatballs and place them on the prepared sheet pan. The meatballs can be prepared ahead of time, covered, and refrigerated for up to 2 days.

RECIPE CONTINUES

4 Place the meatballs in the oven and bake until the internal temperature on an instant-read thermometer inserted into the meat is 165°F, 8 to 10 minutes. Remove from the oven and set aside.

5 Make the sauce: Place the cinnamon stick, black pepper, green and black cardamom pods, dried fenugreek, star anise pod, coriander seeds, and cumin seeds in a small pan without oil. Toast the spices over medium-high heat until they're fragrant but not burned, 1 to 2 minutes. Place the toasted spices in a food processor or spice grinder and process until very fine, 3 to 5 minutes.

6 Heat the ghee in a 5-quart pot over medium heat. Once the ghee is hot and shimmering, add the chopped onions and sauté until tender, about 5 minutes. Add the onion powder, ground cardamom, garam masala, and ground spices from Step 5. Continue to sauté until the spices are fragrant, about 5 minutes more.

7 Add the tomato puree, tomato paste, chicken stock, and cashew flour. Bring the sauce to a simmer and cook, uncovered and stirring frequently, until reduced by half, about 45 minutes.

8 Remove sauce from the heat. Whisk together the cornstarch and $1/2$ cup of water in a small bowl, until a smooth slurry is formed. Add the slurry to the sauce and stir to combine. Bring to a boil over high heat and boil for 1 minute. For a smoother sauce, let it cool slightly, carefully puree it in a blender, and strain it, if desired. Return the sauce to the pot.

9 Add the meatballs to the sauce and cook until they're warm, about 10 minutes. Garnish with cilantro, scallions, and a pinch of flaky Himalayan salt. Serve immediately.

THE GEOGRAPHY OF SALT
Believed to be the most natural and beneficial form of sodium, Himalayan pink salt is akin to table salt save for its striking pigment, its unrefined nature, and a few trace minerals. Slabs of Himalayan pink salt can be used for cooking, curing, and serving food. Whether it is heated or chilled, the block infuses dishes (although not dry foods) with a light salty taste.

KANAWA CURRY

Squid curry with tamarind
and bird's-eye chile

⟨ SERVES 6 TO 8 AS A MAIN DISH ⟩

S ri Lanka turns curry up a notch with spices. This dish calls for 10 curry leaves, plus mustard seeds and cardamom. The tamarind paste adds a touch of sweetness. It can be found at Asian markets or online. As Sri Lanka is an island nation, adding seafood is a no-brainer. This recipe draws inspiration from a squid curry popular in Jaffna, a large city at Sri Lanka's northern tip.

1½ teaspoons fennel seeds

8 green cardamom pods

1 cinnamon stick

1 tablespoon tamarind paste

⅔ cup, plus 1 tablespoon, vegetable oil

1 cup finely chopped white onion

1 green bird's-eye chile (see page xvii), chopped

½ teaspoon mustard seeds

½ teaspoon ground cumin

1 tablespoon minced fresh ginger

5 garlic cloves, peeled and thinly sliced

10 curry leaves (see page xvii)

2 plum tomatoes, finely chopped

1 tablespoon curry powder

1 tablespoon tomato paste

1 tablespoon kosher salt

1 russet potato, diced

1 pound squid, cut into 1-inch thick slices

Cooked basmati rice, for serving

1 Place the fennel seeds, cardamom pods, and cinnamon stick in a small, dry skillet over medium-low heat. Carefully toast the spices until they become very fragrant, 4 to 5 minutes. Remove the pan from heat and grind the spices into a powder in a food processor or spice grinder. Set aside.

2 Place 1 cup of water in a small saucepan. Bring it to a boil over high heat, then add the tamarind paste and stir until it is dissolved. Set aside.

3 Pour ⅓ cup of the vegetable oil into a 4-quart saucepan and place it over medium-high heat. When the oil is hot, stir in the onion and chile and cook until the onion is soft, about 5 minutes.

RECIPE CONTINUES

4   Lower the heat to medium and stir in the mustard seeds and cumin, coating the onion and chile thoroughly. Cook until the spices become fragrant, 1 to 2 minutes. Stir in the ginger and garlic and cook for another 2 to 3 minutes, being careful to not let anything burn.

5   Stir in the curry leaves and let them warm through, about 2 minutes. Add the chopped tomatoes and cook until they soften, about 5 minutes.

6   Quickly stir in the curry powder and tomato paste. Cook for another 5 minutes, lowering the heat if you find that the spices are sticking too much to the bottom of the pot.

7   Stir in the dissolved tamarind paste, plus 4 more cups of water and the salt. Raise the heat to high, bring to a boil, then reduce the heat to low. Cover the pot and simmer to let the flavors meld, 30 minutes.

8   While the curry is simmering, line a plate with paper towels.

9   Pour 1/3 cup of the oil into a large nonstick skillet and place over medium-high heat. When the oil is hot, stir in the potato. Fry the potato until golden brown, about 10 minutes. Using a slotted spoon, transfer the potato to the towel-lined plate and set aside.

10   Drain the skillet. Pour the remaining 1 tablespoon of oil in the skillet and place it over medium-high heat. Stir in the squid pieces and sauté until some begin to brown, about 10 minutes. Remove from the heat and set aside.

11   When the curry is done simmering, carefully pour it into a blender, working in batches if necessary, and pulse until smooth. Return the curry to the pot, then stir in the fried potato and squid. Cook until everything is heated through, about 5 minutes. Stir in the roasted spice powder from Step 1. Remove from the heat.

12   Spoon the curry over basmati rice and serve immediately.

CHU LA

Ground chicken curry

SERVES 6 TO 8 AS A MAIN DISH

A medley of South Asian spices takes center stage in this chicken curry. You can find Kashmiri chiles and fresh curry leaves at Asian specialty stores. If you end up with extra curry leaves, they are perfect for freezing for future use.

2 dried Kashmiri chiles (see page xviii)

¼ cup olive oil

1 pinch asafetida powder (see page xvi)

2 bird's-eye chiles (see page xvii)

1 bay leaf

4 curry leaves (see page xvii)

1 tablespoon dried fenugreek leaves (see page xvii)

2 tablespoons ground turmeric

1 cup chopped yellow onion

2 tablespoons chopped fresh ginger

4 garlic cloves, peeled and minced

2 cups chopped plum tomatoes

1 tablespoon kosher salt

½ cup plain yogurt

1 cup frozen green peas

2 pounds ground chicken

6 tablespoons unsalted butter

1 tablespoon freshly ground black pepper

1 tablespoon ground cinnamon

1 tablespoon ground cumin

1 tablespoon chili powder

1 tablespoon garam masala

¼ cup chopped fresh cilantro leaves

1   Grind the Kashmiri chiles into a powder in a small food processor or spice grinder. Set aside.

2   Heat the olive oil in a large pot over medium heat. Once the oil is hot, add the asafetida powder, bird's-eye chiles, bay leaf, curry leaves, dried fenugreek, 1 tablespoon of the turmeric, and the onion. Stir everything together and sauté until the onion is tender, about 5 minutes.

3   Add the ginger and garlic to the pot. Sauté until they begin to brown, about 5 minutes, and then add the tomatoes and 1½ teaspoons of the salt. Reduce the heat to low and cook for 5 minutes more. Remove from the heat.

4   Transfer the onion and spice mixture to a food processor. Reserve the pot. Add the yogurt to the food processor and pulse until a paste is formed, about 30 seconds. Set aside.

5 Place the peas in the reserved pot over medium heat. Cook the peas until they are thawed, about 1 minute. Add the ground chicken and 1 cup of water, stirring well, then add the butter and cook until it is melted, about 5 minutes.

6 Add the remaining 1 tablespoon of turmeric and the ground Kashmiri chiles to the chicken. Stir everything together, cover the pot, and reduce the heat to low. Cook for 10 minutes.

7 Stir in the black pepper, cinnamon, cumin, chili powder, and remaining 1½ teaspoons of salt. Once everything is incorporated, stir in the yogurt paste. Cook, covered, for 10 minutes more.

8 Remove the pot from the heat and stir in the garam masala and cilantro. Serve immediately.

CURRY AS CATCHALL

Though people worldwide cite curry as their favorite dish from the Indian subcontinent, it has never been a part of native Indian cuisine or language. The name is a transliteration of *kari*, a Tamil word denoting a sauce or relish for rice that morphed into a catchall term for Indian food when the Portuguese came searching for spices in 1498. This generalization became Anglicized in Colonial India when "curry" surfaced—a term meant to encompass all of India's nuanced ingredients and dishes. In doing so, the specificity of dishes such as *dum aloo*, *malai kofta*, and *matar paneer* were lost. The British rendition of curry powder is similar. Inspired by the North Indian spice blend garam masala, it is a pre-mixed combination of popular Indian spices—turmeric, cumin, ginger, coriander, fenugreek, dry mustard, black pepper, chilies, cardamom, and so on.

As curry was introduced in other regions—including the Caribbean islands, Thailand, Malaysia, Indonesia, Cambodia, Sri Lanka, Pakistan, and Japan—it was further adapted and altered. The South African region of Durban, home to the largest population of Indians outside of India, has been developing curry variations since the late 1800s. *Karahi* (such as the chicken version on page 134) is a traditional North Indian, Pakistani, and Afghan dish that evokes popular notions of chicken curry.

CARNE MECHADA

*Venezuelan shredded skirt steak
with sliced peppers and onions*

⊰ SERVES 4 TO 6 AS A MAIN DISH ⊱

Carne mechada, or Venezuelan shredded beef, is the base for many dishes in the South American country, including *pabellón criollo,* a traditional meal with beans, plantains, and rice. But the beef can be used to top arepas and cachapas (page 19) and can be rolled into empanadas as well. Here, it's served simply to allow the flavor of the beef to shine through.

2 pounds skirt steak	1 tablespoon ground cumin	5 cups chicken stock
2 tablespoons olive oil	1 cup diced plum tomato	Kosher salt and freshly ground black pepper
1 cup sliced yellow onion	1 can (28 ounces) crushed Italian tomatoes	Fried Plantains (page 148), for serving (optional)
2 garlic cloves, peeled and minced	1 tablespoon Worcestershire sauce	
1 cup sliced red bell pepper		

1 Slice the steak into ten large pieces and set aside.

2 Heat the olive oil in a stockpot over medium heat. Once the oil is hot, add the onion and garlic and sauté until they are golden brown, about 10 minutes. Add the red bell pepper and cumin and cook for another 2 to 3 minutes.

3 Slowly stir in the diced tomato, crushed tomatoes, and Worcestershire sauce. Add the steak and pour in the stock. Reduce the heat to low and simmer, covered, until the beef is very tender, at least 1½ hours. Add salt and pepper to taste.

4 Remove the meat from the pot and shred it with two forks. Spoon the sauce over the top and add the plantains on the side, if desired. Serve hot.

FRIED PLANTAINS

Sticky-sweet slices of caramelized fruit

Though they look similar, plantains are starchier and less sweet than the everyday Cavendish yellow banana. When they're still green, plantains can be cooked like a starchy vegetable. But when they're allowed to ripen to deep yellow or black, the starches turn to sugar and the plantains are perfect for deep- or pan-frying. The fried plantains can be eaten as a side to a main meal or sweetened for dessert. To prep plantains, cut off both ends and slice the skin from end to end to allow for an easier time peeling. These instructions are for pan-frying; if you want to deep-fry in a Dutch oven, the oil should be at 375°F.

| 1 cup vegetable oil | 4 very ripe plantains, peeled and cut into thick slices | Kosher salt |

1 Place a double layer of paper towels on a large plate and set aside.

2 Place the oil in a medium nonstick skillet over high heat. Let the oil heat for 5 minutes. When you can see the oil moving, drop in a plantain slice—it should bubble vigorously when added.

3 Lower the heat to medium to maintain the temperature and carefully add about ⅓ cup of plantain slices in a single layer using a slotted spoon. Fry the plantains until the edges begin to brown, about 3 minutes. Using the slotted spoon or a spatula, flip the slices and fry until golden brown, about 3 minutes more. You don't want to flip the plantains more than twice. Remove with a slotted spoon and drain on the towel-lined plate. Repeat with the remaining plantain slices, working in batches.

4 Sprinkle the fried plantains with a pinch of salt (or to taste) and serve immediately.

CHEF HÉCTOR

THE EAT OFFBEAT COMMUNITY INVOLVES MORE THAN JUST THE CHEFS. Héctor Arguinzones rarely steps foot into the Long Island City kitchen, and even then only as an intern, but he's nonetheless a part of the collective. Like a few other members of the Eat Offbeat family, Héctor didn't realize his passion for food and being in the kitchen until he relocated to the United States. Now that he has, he tries to keep his Venezuelan culture alive through food, and is working to help others from his country.

When Héctor, his wife, Niurka, and their six-year-old son came to New York City in 2014, they left behind a business as well as their home in Caracas, Venezuela. While he was waiting for his student visa to be approved, Héctor enrolled in English classes and an informal cooking school. In English classes, he spent time talking about himself and his history in order to learn a new language, and simultaneously, he was learning culinary techniques in order to get a job as a line cook. These experiences helped Héctor become conscious of how central food is to his life and his love for his home country. As a child, he was blessed with a mother, Juana, who was known for her cooking. Though not a professional chef, she was able to prepare classic Venezuelan dishes without looking at a recipe, simply recreating the meals she'd learned from her mother. Young Héctor sometimes helped her in the kitchen—especially around the big *Hallacas* (page 164) production that occurs over the days preceding Christmas—but he was more often just observing her style and cooking.

Once he reached adulthood, Héctor was fortunate to land a job in the Venezuelan financial industry, a career that required him to travel extensively throughout the country. Whenever he was on the road, he'd find himself heading to the local food markets, where vendors put their regional spin on those classic

> HÉCTOR DIDN'T REALIZE HIS PASSION FOR FOOD AND BEING IN THE KITCHEN UNTIL HE RELOCATED TO THE UNITED STATES. NOW THAT HE HAS, HE TRIES TO KEEP HIS VENEZUELAN CULTURE ALIVE THROUGH FOOD, AND IS WORKING TO HELP OTHERS FROM HIS COUNTRY.

dishes. This might mean ceviche made with baby shark, as it's prepared along the Venezuelan coast, or when in the south, close to the Amazonian jungle and Brazil, he'd see dishes made with *morrocoy*, the red-footed tortoise. With the ongoing economic crisis in Venezuela, many of these regional recipes and cuisines are in danger of being lost because of emigration.

Héctor did end up leaving the financial industry. Niurka holds a degree in computer science, and with the internet boom of the late 2000s, they decided to go into business together. The two started a successful consultancy where they created and maintained websites for small Venezuelan businesses, often clothing shops. Times were good for the business until the economy began collapsing. Hyperinflation affected every aspect of life in Venezuela, ultimately causing Héctor and Niurka to close their consultancy and leave the country. After moving to New York, Niurka was able to transfer her experience into a role as a website coordinator, monitoring and creating content for bilingual publications.

After taking culinary classes and deciding that he would like to work in food somehow, Héctor met Chef Juan and Manal through the IRC. Because he's on a student visa, he's not legally allowed to work, but he can intern, as he has done for Eat Offbeat, as well as for a few restaurants around town. While he waits for his immigration status to change, he keeps busy with classes and serving New York's burgeoning Venezuelan community. He organizes monthly informational meetings that often turn into potlucks. For those who attend, it's one way to keep learning about their home, giving them an opportunity to experience their favorite foods in a different region's style. Around the holidays, they go all out. One year, Héctor negotiated with a bakery to allow someone to use their kitchen to bake the traditional *Pan de Jamón* (ham and olive bread), while others got together to undertake the considerable hallaca production. And though it is at times very hard to think of the bounty in America when people back home are starving, it's creating meals like this that renews Héctor and his family's spirit and helps them adjust to life in New York.

BEEF KEBAB

Grilled kebab with pomegranate and roasted tomato sauce

◁ **MAKES 20 KEBABS** ▷

The kebab is one of the most recognizable Afghan dishes. Invented by the Turks, it first appeared in Afghanistan during the Ottoman Empire. Now, kebabs are popular throughout the country and are a common street food. This version, like most, is unskewered and easy to grill up. If you find that you need an extra carb for your meal, add a few pieces of fresh naan (Indian flatbread) to the table.

FOR THE SAUCE

3 plum tomatoes or tomatoes on the vine

1 medium yellow onion, peeled

3 tablespoons pomegranate molasses (see page xviii)

2 cups fresh flat-leaf parsley leaves

1½ teaspoons kosher salt

FOR THE KEBABS

1 pound ground beef (80% lean)

1 cup finely chopped fresh flat-leaf parsley leaves

½ cup finely chopped white onion

2 teaspoons kosher salt

2 teaspoons freshly ground black pepper

Cooking spray, for preparing the grill pan

Pomegranate seeds (see box on page 137), for garnish

1 Preheat the oven to 400°F. Line a sheet pan with parchment paper.

2 Make the sauce: Cut the tomatoes and yellow onion into quarters and place them on the prepared sheet pan. Roast them, flipping halfway through, until they have browned, about 20 minutes. Let cool briefly.

3 Place the roasted tomatoes and onion in a food processor and pulse until smooth, about 1 minute. Pour in the pomegranate molasses and pulse again until fully blended, about 1 minute.

4 Add the 2 cups of parsley and the 1½ teaspoons of salt to the food processor. Pulse until the parsley is blended in and the sauce is smooth. Set sauce aside.

5 Make the kebabs: Mix the ground beef, 1 cup of chopped parsley, white onion, salt, and black pepper in a large mixing bowl with your hands.

6 Measure out 2 tablespoons of the beef mixture and form it into an oblong shape, about 3 inches long by 1 inch wide. Repeat with the remaining beef mixture and place the kebabs on a plate until you are ready to cook them.

7   Coat a nonstick grill pan with cooking spray and place it over medium-high heat. Place the kebabs on the grill, working in batches if necessary, and let cook, gently turning every few minutes. The kebabs are done when they are no longer pink and their internal temperature is 160°F, about 10 minutes.

8   Serve the kebabs topped with spoonfuls of the sauce and sprinkle with pomegranate seeds.

NARGES KEBAB

Soft-boiled egg enrobed in spiced beef

‹ MAKES 12 KEBABS ›

Narges kebab is the South Asian version of the Scotch egg—or vice versa, as this recipe may predate the version native to the United Kingdom. The key here is to buy *medium*—not large—eggs. Be extra careful when sliding the assembled kebabs into the deep fryer, as agitation can cause the coating to fall off.

12 medium eggs, plus 1 lightly beaten large egg

½ cup yellow lentils, rinsed and drained

1 russet potato, peeled and quartered

2 pounds ground beef (80% lean)

½ cup finely diced yellow onion

1 tablespoon finely chopped fresh ginger

8 garlic cloves, peeled and minced

½ cup finely chopped fresh cilantro leaves

1 tablespoon kosher salt

2 teaspoons Spice Blend (recipe follows)

Vegetable oil, for deep-frying

Ginger-Tomato Sauce, for serving (recipe follows)

1 Fill a large bowl with cold water and ice cubes. Place the 12 medium eggs in a large pot, cover with water to a depth of 2 inches, and place over medium-high heat. Boil the eggs until soft-boiled, about 6 minutes, then immediately transfer them to the prepared ice bath. When they're cool, peel the eggs.

2 Bring 1 cup of water to a boil in a small saucepan over high heat. Stir in the lentils and lower the heat to a simmer. Cook until the lentils are very tender and the water is absorbed, about 15 minutes.

3 While the lentils are cooking, fill another small saucepan with water and bring it to a boil over high heat. Add the potato and cook until fork-tender, about 15 minutes. Drain and add to the lentils. Mash the lentils and potatoes together.

4 Place the beef, onion, ginger, garlic, cilantro, salt, Spice Blend, and beaten egg in a large mixing bowl. Combine thoroughly with your hands. Add the potato-lentil mash to the beef mixture and mix well to combine thoroughly.

5 Carefully wrap the meat mixture—about ½ cup per egg—around the peeled soft-boiled eggs, covering each egg completely. Set them aside on a platter.

6   Pour the oil into a large heavy-bottomed stockpot or Dutch oven to a depth of at least 2 inches and clip a candy thermometer to the side, making sure it doesn't touch the bottom. Heat the oil to 375°F over high heat, then lower the heat to medium to maintain the temperature during frying. While the oil is heating up, line a large plate with paper towels.

7   Carefully place 2 or 3 kebabs in the oil with a slotted spoon and fry them until they are deep brown, about 15 minutes. Remove them with the slotted spoon and set them on the towel-lined plate. Repeat to fry the remaining kebabs. Let the kebabs cool for 10 minutes, then serve with Ginger-Tomato Sauce.

SPICE BLEND

◄ MAKES 2 TABLESPOONS ►

1 teaspoon ground turmeric

1 teaspoon red chile powder

1 teaspoon ground coriander

1 teaspoon freshly ground black pepper

1 teaspoon garam masala

1 teaspoon ground cumin

Mix the turmeric, red chile powder, coriander, black pepper, garam masala, and cumin together in a bowl.

GINGER-TOMATO SAUCE

◄ MAKES 4 CUPS ►

3 tablespoons vegetable oil

¾ cup chopped yellow onion

4 garlic cloves, peeled and chopped

2 teaspoons Spice Blend (recipe above)

1 tablespoon finely chopped fresh ginger

2 cups diced plum tomatoes

2 cups vegetable stock

1 Heat the oil in a medium saucepan over medium heat. Once the oil is hot, stir in the onion and sauté until tender, about 7 minutes.

2 Stir in the garlic and cook for 3 minutes. Add the Spice Blend and cook, stirring until fragrant, about 1 minute. Stir in the ginger and tomatoes, cooking until the tomatoes are soft, about 5 minutes. Stir in the vegetable stock, cook for 15 minutes more, and remove from the heat.

CHEF RACHANA ❄ NEPAL

CHARI CURRY

Chicken curry with ginger, garlic, and garam masala

⟨ SERVES 4 TO 6 AS A MAIN DISH ⟩

Golden chicken thighs coated in a spicy sauce make this a great weeknight curry. Be careful when sautéing the spices; cumin seeds can burn quickly.

¼ cup olive oil

2 teaspoons fenugreek seeds (see page xvii)

1½ teaspoons cumin seeds

1 teaspoon ground turmeric

3 or 4 curry leaves (see page xvii)

4 teaspoons ground ginger

5 garlic cloves, peeled and finely minced

2 pounds skinless, boneless chicken thighs, cut into ½-inch cubes

1 cup finely chopped yellow onion

1 cup finely chopped red bell pepper

4 teaspoons ground cumin

4 teaspoons ground coriander

1 teaspoon chili powder

1 teaspoon freshly ground black pepper

1 teaspoon garam masala

1 tablespoon kosher salt

2 cups finely chopped plum tomatoes

1 cup plain yogurt

5 tablespoons finely chopped fresh cilantro leaves, for garnish

1 Heat the olive oil in a large pot over high heat. When the oil is hot, add the fenugreek seeds. When the fenugreek seeds darken, add the cumin seeds, turmeric, curry leaves, ginger, and garlic and fry until fragrant, 3 to 5 minutes. Add the chicken cubes and cook until they're golden brown and cooked through, 15 to 17 minutes. Place the chicken in a bowl and refrigerate, covered, until Step 5.

2 Add the onion and bell pepper to the same pot and sauté over medium-high heat until the onion is tender, about 5 minutes. Add the ground cumin, coriander, chili powder, black pepper, garam masala, and salt. Stir together and cook until spices are fragrant, about 3 minutes.

3 Add the tomatoes and cook for 5 minutes. Add 2 cups of water, lower the heat to medium, and cook until the sauce is reduced, about 15 minutes. Cool slightly.

4 Working in batches, carefully place the sauce in a blender and puree until smooth. Return the sauce to the pot and stir in the chicken. Cook over medium heat until warmed through, about 10 minutes. Stir in the yogurt.

5 Serve garnished with the chopped cilantro.

—MNAZZALEH—

Eggplants stuffed with beef and pine nuts

⟨ SERVES 4 TO 6 AS A MAIN DISH ⟩

The key to this dish is getting the correct type of eggplant. You'll want to use Indian eggplants, which are small, round, and purple and look similar to baby globe or Italian eggplants. You can also experiment with small, green Thai eggplants, which are about the same size as Indian eggplants. The water that's poured into the dish in Step 7 is simply to keep the eggplants from sticking. If you notice it has boiled away in the oven, quickly pour a little bit more in.

10 small Indian eggplants

Vegetable oil, for frying

2 medium yellow onions, peeled and finely chopped

1 pound ground beef (80% lean)

1 teaspoon seven spices (see page xix)

1 teaspoon kosher salt

½ teaspoon freshly ground black pepper

1 tablespoon olive oil

1 medium tomato, sliced

⅓ cup pine nuts, for garnish

White or whole wheat pita, for serving

Sliced green bell pepper, for garnish (optional)

1 With the stem still attached, make a slit in each eggplant vertically—start at the bottom and cut about three quarters of the way up to the top.

2 Pour the oil into a large heavy-bottomed stockpot or Dutch oven to a depth of at least 2 inches and clip a candy thermometer to the side, making sure it doesn't touch the bottom. Heat the oil to 350°F over high heat, then lower the heat to medium to maintain the temperature during frying. While the oil is heating up, line a large plate with paper towels.

3 Carefully slide each eggplant into the oil using a slotted spoon or mesh strainer. Working in batches of 3 or 4, deep-fry the eggplants until the inside of the eggplant is cooked and tender, 12 to 15 minutes. Carefully remove with the mesh strainer and place on the towel-lined plate.

4 Place the onions, ground beef, seven spices, salt, and pepper in a medium mixing bowl and stir with a wooden spoon to mix well.

RECIPE CONTINUES

5 Preheat the oven to 375° F.

6 Heat 1 tablespoon of oil in a large nonstick skillet over medium-high heat. Add the beef mixture and cook, stirring occasionally, until the meat is browned, 10 to 15 minutes. Remove the pan from the heat and cool slightly.

7 Place a tomato slice inside each eggplant. Carefully spoon the cooked meat into the eggplants, stuffing each until full. Place the stuffed eggplants in a 13 x 9-inch baking dish and carefully pour 1 cup of cold water into the dish. Bake the eggplants until the tops are browned, 10 to 15 minutes.

8 Meanwhile, heat the remaining 1 tablespoon of vegetable oil in a small pan over medium-high heat. When the oil is hot, add the pine nuts. Toast them until they're golden brown, stirring frequently and taking care not to burn them, 2 to 3 minutes.

9 Serve the eggplants with pita bread, topping with pine nuts and sliced green bell pepper, if desired.

CHEF DIAA

SYRIA

WHEN DIAA LEFT SCHOOL AT THE AGE OF 15, HE IMMEDIATELY WENT TO work for his uncle, who runs one of the top five restaurants in Damascus. Because his relative was the owner and head chef, Diaa says with a twinkle in his eye, he didn't have to start at the bottom, dishwashing or prepping vegetables. He began his career as a sous chef, receiving his culinary lessons under the wing of his uncle.

Even though Diaa would spend nine-hour days in this kitchen, seven days a week, he never considered it working overtime. He didn't feel he needed to take time off because he was happy when working, especially when they were busy with customers, filling the restaurant, loving the food, and spreading the word about it so more people came to eat there. He was never tired, he says, because it was such a good job.

Diaa is the exception in the Eat Offbeat kitchen in terms of experience—unlike most of the other chefs, he began his professional culinary career at an early age and has owned several restaurants. He is the fastest prepper and chopper, and the other chefs often learn from him.

In his early twenties, Diaa moved to Russia and started a restaurant there. When asked what's different about serving Syrian food in New York versus in other countries, he says he really appreciates how open and adventurous New Yorkers and Americans are. "They try anything, and then they decide if they like it or not. Most often, they love it. Some tastes they may not. But at least they try."

Before the crisis in Syria began, Diaa was in Sudan with his family, trying to launch a restaurant there. But when he wanted to leave, he couldn't go back to Syria because the war had started. So he went to Jordan instead, thinking the war would end soon, and he'd be able to return to Damascus. He waited four years in Jordan as a refugee before coming to the United States in 2016. He now lives in Staten Island with his wife, two sons, and two daughters.

Diaa has been so successful that he is opening his own restaurant in South Williamsburg, Brooklyn. Although he is sad to be leaving Eat Offbeat, it's exactly the kind of American dream story that Eat Offbeat wants for its chefs.

—HALLACAS—

Steamed banana leaf tamales stuffed with pork and beef

⟨ MAKES 12 TAMALES ⟩

The Venezuelan version of Latin America's beloved tamales, *hallacas*, are typically made in large batches during a day-long process with lots of family around to help. Cornmeal wrappers are filled with beef and pork stew before being sealed into a banana leaf casing and steamed. With such arduous preparation, hallacas are traditionally only served during the Christmas season. You can find frozen banana leaves at international grocery stores. For this recipe, it's important to defrost them in their packaging to keep them from drying out. If you can't find banana leaves, aluminum foil can be used as a substitute.

½ cup soy sauce

½ cup Worcestershire sauce

¼ cup distilled white vinegar

3½ teaspoons fresh thyme leaves

3½ teaspoons dried oregano

2 teaspoons garlic paste

7 tablespoons olive oil

12 ounces pork loin, cut into 1-inch cubes

12 ounces flank steak, cut into 1-inch cubes

1½ cups thinly sliced leeks

1 cup finely chopped red bell pepper

1 cup finely chopped green bell pepper

½ cup finely chopped celery

1 medium white onion, peeled and thinly sliced

¾ cup finely chopped carrot

½ cup chopped fresh flat-leaf parsley leaves

½ cup chopped fresh cilantro leaves

⅓ cup sliced green olives

1 tablespoon grated piloncillo sugar (see page xviii)

2 cups yellow corn flour, plus more as needed

2 cups chicken stock, plus more as needed

3½ teaspoons achiote paste (see page xvi)

2 pounds banana leaves, about 10 by 12 inches each

1   Place the soy sauce, Worcestershire sauce, vinegar, fresh thyme, dried oregano, and garlic paste in a small mixing bowl and whisk to combine.

2   Pour 3 tablespoons of the olive oil into a large saucepan over medium-high heat. When the oil is hot, add the pork and flank steak, stirring to coat. Cook, stirring frequently to keep the meat from sticking to the pan, until the pork has lost its pink color and all of the beef is browned, about 10 minutes. Stir in the soy sauce mixture and lower the heat to medium. Boil until the liquid has reduced by one-third, 17 to 20 minutes. Remove the pan from the heat and set aside.

3   Heat the remaining 4 tablespoons of olive oil in a large nonstick pan over medium heat. Once the oil is hot, add the leeks, red and green bell peppers, celery, onion, and carrot and cook, stirring frequently, until the vegetables are tender, about 20 minutes. Stir in the pork and beef, then the parsley, cilantro, olives, and sugar. Continue cooking to fully dissolve the sugar, warm the meat, and wilt the herbs, about 5 minutes. Remove the pot from the heat and let cool for at least 15 minutes.

4   Place the corn flour and chicken stock in a medium mixing bowl and stir until a stiff dough forms. Add more liquid or corn flour as needed.

5   Place the achiote paste in a small skillet over medium heat and cook until it melts, about 2 minutes. Remove the pan from the heat and stir 3 teaspoons of the melted paste into the corn flour dough until fully incorporated.

6   Place a banana leaf on a flat surface. Keep a damp cloth over the other defrosted banana leaves to keep them from drying out. Brush a small amount of the remaining melted achiote paste in a small 4-inch circle in the center of the banana leaf. Place a small pancake of dough over the circle and add 2 tablespoons of the meat in the middle of the pancake.

7   Carefully fold the left third of the banana leaf along the veins, forcing the pancake of dough to fold over the meat. Then fold the right third over the meat and other side of pancake, fully enveloping the meat with the dough. Fold the top and bottom over the seam. Place another banana leaf on your work surface and place the tamale inside, flat side facing up. Fold this banana leaf over the tamale with the same folding pattern. Repeat with a third leaf and, if needed, a fourth, until the outside leaf has no cracks—it needs to be waterproof. Once you've achieved that, cut a strip from another banana leaf and use it to form a belt around the tamale, then tie the entire tamale with baker's string. Repeat with remaining filling, dough, and banana leaves.

8   Place a steamer basket in a large stockpot and add water to reach just below the bottom of the basket. Place over medium-high heat, bring to a boil, and lower the heat to a simmer. Carefully place the tamales in the steamer basket. Cover the stockpot and steam until tamales are firm to the touch, about 1 hour. Remove from the steamer and serve immediately.

EGYPTIAN MOUSSAKA

Baked eggplant and ground beef with béchamel sauce

⊰ **SERVES 6 TO 8 AS A MAIN DISH** ⊱

Mitslal learned this dish while working in Egypt. This version of the layered dish is eggplant-based with ground beef. You'll want to save this hearty dish for winter weekends when you have the time for a great Sunday dinner.

4 eggplants (about 2½ pounds)

Canola oil, for deep-frying

2 tablespoons olive oil

3 cups chopped white onions

2 tablespoons tomato paste

2 garlic cloves, peeled and minced

1½ tablespoons finely chopped fresh ginger

1 can (15 ounces) peeled tomatoes, crushed by hand

1½ pounds ground beef (80% lean)

Cooking spray, for preparing the grill pan

2 tablespoons cornstarch

4 cups whole milk

2 tablespoons Maggi Hot & Sweet Tomato Chilli Sauce (see page xviii)

5 ounces Gorgonzola cheese, crumbled

1 tablespoon kosher salt

1 tablespoon freshly ground black pepper

Chopped fresh dill and cilantro, for garnish (optional)

1 Stem and peel 3 of the eggplants and cut crosswise into ½-inch-thick slices.

2 Pour the canola oil into a large heavy-bottomed stockpot or Dutch oven to a depth of at least 2 inches and clip a candy thermometer to the side, making sure it doesn't touch the bottom. Heat the oil to 375°F over high heat, then lower the heat to medium to maintain the temperature during frying. While the oil is heating up, line a large plate with paper towels.

3 Use a slotted spoon or mesh strainer to carefully slide 4 eggplant slices into the oil. Push the slices around, making sure both sides fry until golden brown, about 1 minute per side. Quickly remove the fried slices with the slotted spoon or strainer and place them on the towel-lined plate. Continue to fry batches of eggplant, placing paper towels between the layers on the plate. Set aside.

4 Make the meat filling: Pour 1 tablespoon of the olive oil into a large nonstick skillet and place over medium heat. When the oil is hot, add 2 cups of the chopped

RECIPE CONTINUES

onions and cook, stirring frequently, until the onions are golden brown, about 15 minutes. Reduce the heat to medium-low and stir in the tomato paste, garlic, and ginger. Continue to cook, stirring occasionally, until the ginger and garlic are tender, about 10 minutes.

5 Stir in the crushed tomatoes and cook until the tomatoes are simmering, about 10 minutes. Stir in the ground beef and bring back to a simmer, cover, and cook until the meat is cooked through, about 30 minutes. Remove the pan from the heat.

6 Make the sauce: Spray a nonstick grill pan with cooking spray and place it over medium heat. Grill the remaining whole eggplant, rotating frequently, until slightly collapsed and softened, about 45 minutes. Carefully remove it from the heat and let cool to the touch, about 10 minutes. Cut it in half and use a large spoon to scoop out the insides. Set them aside and discard the skin.

7 Pour the remaining 1 tablespoon of olive oil into a large saucepan and place over medium heat. When the oil is hot, stir in the remaining 1 cup of onions. Cook until the onions are translucent, about 10 minutes, and then stir in the grilled eggplant to combine. Stir in the cornstarch until thoroughly incorporated, then whisk in 2 cups of the milk. Cook, whisking continuously, for 5 minutes. Then whisk in the remaining 2 cups of milk and continue to whisk until the milk begins to simmer, about 10 minutes more. Don't let the milk boil.

8 Whisk in the Maggi sauce, then stir in the Gorgonzola cheese. Once the cheese has melted, about 5 minutes, add the salt and pepper. Remove from the heat and let cool slightly.

9 Preheat the oven to 400°F. Lightly spray a 13 x 9-inch baking dish with cooking spray.

10 Build the moussaka: Spoon enough meat filling into the prepared dish to cover the bottom. Top the filling with a layer of the fried eggplant. Repeat the layers again, ending with a layer of fried eggplant. Then carefully spoon the sauce over the moussaka.

11 Bake until the top is golden brown, about 45 minutes. Let cool for 10 minutes, garnish with the dill and cilantro, if desired, then cut into squares and serve.

— CHICKEN CILANTRO —

Mustard-and-lemon–marinated chicken with cilantro

⟨ **SERVES 4 AS A MAIN DISH** ⟩

This Senegalese entrée is perfect for an easy weeknight dinner. The Dijon mustard and lemon juice give the chicken a wonderful piquant flavor. Mariama might serve it with rice and a salad of tomato, lettuce, and cucumber.

⅓ cup, plus 3 tablespoons, olive oil

3 tablespoons fresh lemon juice

5 teaspoons minced garlic

1 cup fresh cilantro leaves

2 chicken bouillon cubes

1 tablespoon Dijon mustard

3 teaspoons freshly ground black pepper

2 teaspoons paprika

2½ teaspoons kosher salt

2 pounds boneless, skinless chicken thighs

2 cups sliced yellow onions

2 cups sliced red bell peppers

1 tablespoon distilled white vinegar

1 Preheat the oven to 400°F. Line a sheet pan with parchment paper.

2 Place 3 tablespoons of the olive oil, the lemon juice, 3 teaspoons of the garlic, the cilantro, 1 bouillon cube, the mustard, 2 teaspoons of the black pepper, the paprika, and 1½ teaspoons of the salt in a medium mixing bowl. Whisk everything together, breaking down the bouillon cube, until fully incorporated. Add the chicken to the bowl and stir to coat it thoroughly.

3 Spread out the chicken on the prepared sheet pan and bake until the chicken is golden and has reached an internal temperature of 160°F on an instant-read thermometer, about 30 minutes. Set it aside.

4 Place the remaining ⅓ cup of olive oil in a pot over medium heat. Once the oil is hot, add the onions, bell peppers, the remaining 2 teaspoons of garlic, the remaining 1 teaspoon of black pepper, and the remaining bouillon cube. Cook, stirring occasionally, until the onions and peppers are tender, about 10 minutes.

5 Stir in the vinegar and the 1 teaspoon of remaining salt. Cook until the vegetables are extremely tender, about 5 minutes more. Stir in the chicken and ⅓ cup of water. Reduce the heat to low and simmer until the chicken is heated through, about 10 minutes. Serve.

CHEF DHUHA ✳ IRAQ

CHICKEN SHAWARMA

Roasted chicken in shawarma-spiced yogurt sauce

⊰ SERVES 4 TO 6 AS A MAIN DISH ⊱

Chicken shawarma is great for an easy weeknight meal that's more flavorful than baked chicken breast. Shawarma spice blends can be found at specialty grocers, but since they're made from readily available spices, you can make your own in a pinch (numerous recipes can be found on the internet).

1 pound skinless, boneless chicken thighs, cut into 1-inch cubes	½ cup diced plum tomato	1 cup chicken stock
	1 teaspoon tomato paste	2 teaspoons shawarma spices (see page xix)
1 tablespoon olive oil	1 teaspoon pepper paste (see Note)	
1 cup diced yellow onion		1 teaspoon kosher salt
1 teaspoon ground cumin	1 teaspoon distilled white vinegar	½ cup plain yogurt

1 Preheat the oven to 400°F. Line a sheet pan with parchment paper.

2 Place the chicken cubes on the prepared sheet pan. Roast the chicken until golden brown, about 30 minutes. Remove from the oven and set aside.

3 While the chicken is cooking, heat the olive oil in a large pot over medium-high heat. When the oil is hot, add the onion and cumin and sauté until the onion is tender, 5 to 8 minutes. Remove from the heat and let cool slightly.

4 Put the onion, tomato, tomato paste, pepper paste, vinegar, chicken stock, shawarma spices, salt, and yogurt in a food processor. Pulse until the sauce is smooth.

5 Return the sauce to the pot, stir in the chicken, and place over medium heat. Simmer until the sauce reduces and thickens, about 20 minutes. Serve immediately.

NOTE Sometimes referred to as sweet pepper paste or red pepper paste, this ingredient is essentially a thick puree of roasted red peppers. It's available in Middle Eastern grocery stores or online.

FEASTING IN THE MIDDLE EAST

Shawarma, a hallmark of Levantine cuisine, is a globally beloved street food. It is considered the most common sandwich in several Middle Eastern regions, including Iraq, where it is referred to as *guss*. Origins can be traced to the Turkish dish *döner kebab*, which arose during the Ottoman Empire in the nineteenth century, following the invention of the vertical rotisserie. Though flame-broiled meat paired with flatbread existed prior to this, the move from a horizontal spit refined the roasting process and allowed the meat's fat to be retained. Shawarma's etymology stems from the Turkish word *çevirme* ("turning"), which speaks to the most integral aspect of its production. The cooking process involves stacking seasoned meat—lamb, chicken, beef, veal, goat, or turkey—on a vertical spit, where it forms a conical shape that is slowly turned and roasted for hours. As the meat rotates on the rotisserie, thin slices are cleaved from the cooked portion. Theatrics are a key element in serving Syrian shawarma; in street stalls and restaurants, cooks clad in all-white outfits make a show out of their meat-cutting prowess.

Accompaniments vary by region, but shawarma is typically served in pita bread with sour pickles, diced vegetables, and tahini sauce. In Damascus, *khubz*—round, unleavened flatbread moistened with the meat's juices—is served. The spices used to season shawarma vary as well but generally include coriander, turmeric, cardamom, paprika, cumin, and cinnamon.

POULET YASSA

Marinated roast chicken with onions and olives

⊰ SERVES 4 TO 6 AS A MAIN DISH ⊱

Chicken *yassa* came into being in the southern Senegalese region of Casamance, which lies between Gambia and Guinea-Bissau. Be careful when handling the Scotch bonnet pepper and make sure to avoid touching your eyes after mincing it. For less heat, remove the seeds.

1½ pounds boneless, skinless chicken thighs, cut into 1-inch cubes

2 tablespoons garlic paste

1½ chicken bouillon cubes

4 teaspoons freshly ground black pepper

3 teaspoons kosher salt

2 tablespoons fresh lemon juice

7½ teaspoons Dijon mustard

2 tablespoons distilled white vinegar

4 cups sliced yellow onions

½ cup olive oil

1 Scotch bonnet pepper, minced

½ cup sliced Spanish olives

Cooked rice, for serving

1 Combine the chicken, 1 tablespoon of the garlic paste, ½ of a bouillon cube, 3 teaspoons of the black pepper, 1½ teaspoons of salt, 1 tablespoon of lemon juice, and 3 teaspoons of the mustard in a medium mixing bowl. Cover the bowl and marinate in the refrigerator for at least 10 hours or overnight.

2 Preheat the oven to 400°F. Line a sheet pan with parchment paper. Spread the chicken on the prepared sheet pan and bake until it is slightly golden, about 20 minutes. Remove the chicken from the oven and set aside.

3 Combine the remaining garlic paste, bouillon cube, black pepper, salt, lemon juice, mustard, and vinegar in a medium mixing bowl and whisk to combine. Break the bouillon cube apart as you whisk. Add the onions and stir to coat thoroughly.

4 Heat the olive oil in a large saucepan over medium heat. Add the Scotch bonnet pepper and let it sizzle until fragrant, about 10 seconds, then stir in the onion mixture. Cook, stirring, about 20 minutes. Stir in 1 cup of water and the cooked chicken with its juices. Reduce the heat to medium-low, cover the pot, and cook until the onions are very tender and the sauce has thickened, about 15 minutes.

5 Stir in the olives and let it rest, off the heat, for 10 minutes before serving with rice.

CHEF MARIAMA

SENEGAL

IT TOOK CHEF MARIAMA SOME TIME TO WARM UP TO THE EAT OFFBEAT kitchen—she had never worked before, and was a bit shy at first—but make no mistake, she's no stranger to togetherness. Born and raised in Senegal, Mariama has always been surrounded by a large family. Growing up, it was her mother, her father, his two other wives, and her siblings. When she married her husband at seventeen, his family of more than twenty-five people became hers as well. Her spouse and their five children, whose ages range from two to sixteen, now constitute her immediate family.

> **"WHEN YOU WANT TO COOK, DON'T MAKE EVERYTHING ALL AT ONCE. JUST DO ONE THING AT A TIME."**

Born and raised in Dakar, Mariama traces her culinary origins back to her mother, who began teaching her the tricks of the cooking trade when Mariama was nine. From measuring water for rice to haggling at the open-air market that was a twenty-minute walk from their house, she acted as a constant source of guidance and affirmation. The first time Mariama was solely responsible for a meal, her mother enlisted her to cook for her father's brother, who was visiting for lunch. It was a special day, so when Mariama used an excessive amount of water and made the rice too moist, she cried. But her mother was compassionate and patient about it, as were her other family members. Might it be a coincidence that to this day Mariama has an aversion to rice? It might also be that she hails from a nation where jollof (*thiéboudienne*) is the national dish.

Once Mariama moved into the home of her husband's family, the burden of preparing meals fell on her: "You have to cook. And who cooked? Me!" Such a task required a four-day period of nonstop cooking and grocery shopping, followed by a sixteen-day rest period before the cycle began again. Though it may sound intense, Mariama insists that things were easier this way; making daily meals is a newfound, exhausting experience for her. "When you're in Africa, you pay someone to clean your clothes, your house . . . but here you do everything."

After emigrating to New York City in 2011 to join her husband—who had moved there years before—and provide her children with a better education, Mariama found herself stuck in the routine of taking her kids to and from school. Though she was daunted by the thought of solo subway travel and being surrounded by strangers, her husband urged her to change her life by facing her fears and prioritizing her own goals.

A conversation about her life's trajectory with her friend Larissa led Mariama to Eat Offbeat, where Larissa worked. Shortly after, Mariama received a call from Manal, who invited her to come in the next day. From her first shift at Eat Offbeat, she proved herself to be a model employee. "Mariama is always on time," says Manal. "She's always a shiny face in the kitchen. I've never heard Mariama complain about anything."

Since then, she has wholeheartedly devoted herself to Eat Offbeat, working five days a week in between her English courses. Mariama's experience there has widened every aspect of her worldview, from the recipes she uses to her ability to be independent in the city. Her openness to guidance in the kitchen has allowed her to learn a great deal from her teammates—especially Mitslal, Shanthi, and Nasrin, some of the first people to reach out and help her understand different foods. As she's someone who includes chicken in every meal, it's no surprise that her Eat Offbeat specialties are Poulet Yassa (page 172) and Chicken Cilantro (page 169), and her favorite Eat Offbeat dishes are momos and Diaa's shawarma.

Mariama has settled into her New York City life, but there are elements of Senegal that will always remain with her. Religious and familial coexistence are infused in her beliefs; as a Muslim woman, she takes pride in the fact that followers of Islam peacefully coexist with Christians in her nation, with no need for compromise on either side. "It's a big country but we live together—there's no separation." Eating rituals exemplify her culture's communal nature; her family spends mealtime on the floor, using their hands to scoop dishes out of big bowls that starkly contrast the isolated nature of plates on a table. Though she is reserved (and claims she doesn't have much to say), once Mariama opens up, it's easy to see that her actions inside and outside of the kitchen are propelled by her love of cooking and of unity.

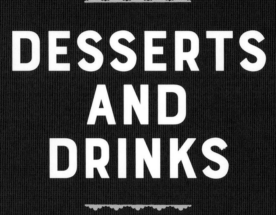

DESSERTS
AND
DRINKS

NASRIN'S TEA

Black tea with Persian rock candy

— 178 —

SHANTHI'S TEA

Milk tea with vanilla and sugar

— 179 —

BASHIR'S DOOGH

Salty yogurt drink with mint

— 182 —

NASRIN'S DOOGH

*Salty yogurt drink
garnished with dried roses*

— 184 —

DATE TRUFFLES

*Jammy, spiced pressed dates
rolled around a walnut center*

— 185 —

SUMAC BROWNIES

Eat Offbeat's take on a spiced brownie

— 187 —

DEGUÉ

Tangy and sweet pudding with millet

— 188 —

BOFLOT

*Fried dough puff puffs rolled
in cinnamon-sugar dust*

— 190 —

ROLLED BAKLAVA

*Sweet phyllo pastry stuffed
with cardamom-spiced pistachios*

— 194 —

CAKE BAKLAVA

*A dry, nutty cake spiced
with cardamom and saffron*

— 196 —

NASRIN'S TEA

Black tea with Persian rock candy

MAKES FOUR 1-CUP SERVINGS

Tea and *châikhânes*, or tea houses, have a special place in Persian culture. A traditional cup of chai involves brewing the tea using a metal samovar. It could be steeped with dried rose petals or a few green cardamom pods. Sugar is added via *nabat*, Persian rock candy infused with saffron threads. Persian black tea with bergamot oil is available online, but in a pinch, you can use a good-quality Earl Grey.

| 1 tablespoon loose-leaf Persian black tea | 4 sticks nabat (Persian rock candy) | Dried edible rose petals, for garnish (optional) |

1 Place 4 cups of water in a small saucepan over high heat. Bring to a boil.

2 Add the tea leaves to the mesh strainer of a teapot. Pour the boiling water into the teapot, add the strainer with leaves, and let the tea steep until the liquid is dark and fragrant, about 5 minutes.

3 Place 1 stick of nabat in each mug. Pour the tea over the top and swirl the nabat so it dissolves.

4 Serve garnished with dried rose petals, if desired.

CHEF SHANTHINI ✳ SRI LANKA

SHANTHI'S TEA

Milk tea with vanilla and sugar

◄ MAKES FOUR 1-CUP SERVINGS ►

As one of the world's largest producers of tea, Sri Lanka, formerly Ceylon, has its own tea culture, though most of the country's tea leaves are exported. "Regular" tea in Sri Lanka comes with milk and sugar. You must specify if you want it served as plain black tea.

2 teaspoons loose black tea or the contents of 2 bags black tea	2 cups whole milk 2 tablespoons sugar	½ teaspoon pure vanilla extract

1 Place 2 cups of water in a small saucepan over high heat. Bring to a boil and add the loose tea. Steep, lowering the heat while maintaining a rolling boil, until the liquid darkens, about 3 minutes.

2 Remove the saucepan from the heat and strain the tea to remove the loose leaves. Set the tea aside.

3 Add the milk to another small saucepan and heat over medium-low heat. Bring to a boil, whisking often to avoid burning the milk. Once the milk is boiling, whisk in the tea, sugar, and vanilla extract. Reduce the heat to low and simmer for 5 minutes.

4 Pour the tea into mugs and serve hot.

CHEF BASHIR

AFGHANISTAN

EVEN THOUGH WOMEN ARE TRADITIONALLY THE COOKS IN AFGHAN HOUSE-holds, Bashir Bakhtyar learned his kitchen skills at an early age from his father, who was a caterer and a butcher. Bashir's childhood was filled with rich culinary experiences—his father would butcher four or five bulls each day—and Bashir acted as junior assistant as his dad catered parties and other weekend events, sometimes for gatherings of more than 1,000 people.

Bashir's journey from the city of Kandahar in Afghanistan was a long one—it was his wife's dying wish that he leave the country with his two sons. After leaving Afghanistan, his family lived on Nauru, a small island nation in Oceania where Australia sends asylum seekers and refugees. Bashir worked as a chef at a restaurant, cooking Afghan cuisine there for three years. When he arrived in New York, he received lots of opportunities and job offers, but after a visit to the Queens kitchen, he knew that Eat Offbeat was the place for him—the team bonding, familial vibe, and cohesion that are integral to the culture felt right to him.

In his current home in Flushing, New York, Bashir pre-pares food for the Afghan community that he met through his mosque, continuing the traditions and keeping alive the skills that he learned from his father. He says, "They want someone to make dishes like fried lamb and *kabuli pulao* because they are tired of eating sandwiches."

Although Bashir says that Afghans don't like spices and don't lean on dried chiles, his signature spice blend—containing dried Kashmiri chiles (see page xviii) and at least twelve other spices—can be seen balancing on a shelf over the chefs' work stations at the kitchen. And his signature dish, Chicken Karahi (page 134), is so fragrant that it imprints a rich scent-memory on anyone who eats—or comes near—it.

> "YOU CAN'T HAVE TWO WATERMELONS IN ONE HAND. ONE OF THEM WILL FALL EVENTUALLY."
>
> —AFGHAN PROVERB

BASHIR'S DOOGH

Salty yogurt drink with mint

B ashir talks about his version of *doogh* when describing the festivities centered around Ramadan. Doogh is the perfect antidote to the oily foods that are traditionally prepared for iftar—if you drink it, you don't get the feeling of having eaten a lot of heavy dishes. The one con, he says, is that you get very drowsy and could sleep for three or four hours after drinking it! In his version, the cooling mint and refreshing cucumber add a hint of flavor.

1 cup plain Greek yogurt

1 tablespoon fresh lemon juice

⅓ cup cold water

½ teaspoon fine sea salt

2 tablespoons diced cucumber

¼ cup dried mint, packed

¾ cup cubed ice

Fresh mint leaves and edible flowers, for garnish (optional)

1   Place the yogurt, lemon juice, water, salt, and cucumber in a blender and pulse until smooth.

2   Add the dried mint to the blender and pulse again until incorporated.

3   Add the ice to the blender and blend on a low speed until all of the ice is crushed.

4   Pour into a glass and serve, garnished with fresh mint leaves and flowers, if desired.

—NASRIN'S DOOGH—

Salty yogurt drink garnished with dried roses

While it didn't make it into culinary literature until the late 1800s, *doogh* has existed in some form since at least 500 CE (and possibly longer). The yogurt-based drink is especially popular on hot summer days when cooling down is all you want to do. Available in a variety of flavors, and sometimes carbonated, this version with fragrant (though optional) dried rose petals comes from Nasrin.

1¾ cups plain Greek yogurt	1 tablespoon fine sea salt	Cubed ice
1⅓ cups sour cream	1 tablespoon dried mint	Dried edible rose petals, for garnish (optional)

1 Place 2 cups of water and the yogurt, sour cream, salt, and dried mint in a half-gallon jar, pitcher, or medium mixing bowl. Stir to combine. Cover with a lid or plastic wrap and place in the refrigerator for at least 3 hours or overnight.

2 Fill four glasses with ice and pour the doogh into each glass. Serve, garnished with dried rose petals, if desired.

IRAN'S SIGNATURE FRAGRANCE

Dried rose petals, known as *gole-e sorkh*, are a popular garnish in Iran. In the Persian plateau and northwestern Iran, ground petals are featured in *advieh*, a spice mixture used atop rice, bean, and chicken dishes. To intensify the richness of the fragrance, the petals may be lightly toasted before use.

Rose petals may also be steeped in simple syrup to create a sweet nectar for infusions. Crushing the petals and mixing the powder with granulated sugar has a similar effect. Regardless of preparation style, dried rose petals leave a fragrant impression on herbal tea, Turkish Delight, jam, harissa paste, doughnuts, biscuits, and shortcakes, or savory dishes like *mast-o khiyar*—yogurt with cucumbers, herbs, walnuts, and raisins.

—DATE TRUFFLES—

Jammy, spiced pressed dates rolled around a walnut center

⟨ **MAKES 24 TRUFFLES** ⟩

Using pressed dates in desserts is common in the Eat Offbeat kitchen. Unlike jam-like date paste, pressed dates have a solid yet malleable texture, almost like fondant or modeling clay. They can also be found labeled as "baking dates" in supermarkets. Because pressed dates are very dense, the only way to truly incorporate all of the ingredients in these truffles is with your hands. As for the nuts, if you don't like walnuts, you can use almonds instead. Date truffles can be kept in the refrigerator, covered, for up to 1 week.

17 ounces pitted, pressed dates	2 teaspoons ground cinnamon	24 walnut halves
1 tablespoon ground cardamom	4 teaspoons olive oil	¼ cup unsweetened cocoa powder

1 Place the dates, cardamom, cinnamon, and olive oil in a medium mixing bowl. Mix the ingredients by hand until well combined.

2 Measure out 1 tablespoon of the date mixture into your hand and wrap it around 1 walnut half. Roll the truffle between your palms to make it into a sphere, enveloping the walnut. Set it aside. Repeat with the remaining date mixture and walnuts.

3 Once all the truffles are made, place the cocoa powder in a shallow dish and roll each truffle in the cocoa powder until fully coated. Serve.

SUMAC BROWNIES

Eat Offbeat's take on a spiced brownie

⟨ MAKES 16 BROWNIES ⟩

Semisweet digestive biscuits are a late nineteenth-century invention, when making cookies with malt was thought to aid digestion. In this unusual brownie recipe—created by Dhuha and Chef Juan as a twist on a typical American dessert—the digestives thicken the melted chocolate and butter to form a batter. The sumac adds a slight sweet-tart flavor to the fudgy brownies.

1 cup (2 sticks) unsalted butter, softened, plus more for greasing the pan

8 ounces semisweet baking chocolate

1¼ cups sugar

½ cup ground sumac (see page xix)

8 ounces (about 15 cookies) digestive biscuits

4 large eggs, lightly beaten

1 Preheat the oven to 375°F. Grease an 8 x 8-inch pan with butter and line it with parchment paper.

2 Place the chocolate in the top of a double boiler set over simmering water on medium-low heat. Carefully stir until it melts, then remove the boiler from the heat and let cool.

3 Place ¼ cup of the sugar and the sumac in a food processor and pulse until fully blended. Pour the sugar mixture into a bowl and set it aside. Place the cookies in the food processor and pulse until they form coarse crumbles, about 2 minutes.

4 Place the 1 cup butter and the remaining 1 cup sugar in a large mixing bowl. Using a hand mixer at medium speed, beat until light and fluffy, about 5 minutes. Beat in the eggs until fully combined, about 2 minutes, then add the cookie crumbles and beat until fully incorporated, about 5 minutes. With the mixer on low, mix in the melted chocolate until fully incorporated, about 5 minutes.

5 Pour the batter into the prepared pan, spreading it evenly and smoothing the top with a spatula. Sprinkle the sugar-sumac mixture over the top of the batter.

6 Bake the brownies until a toothpick inserted into the center comes out clean, 35 to 40 minutes. Let the brownies cool before serving.

– DEGUÉ –

Tangy and sweet pudding with millet

⟨ SERVES 6 ⟩

D egué, or *thiakry*, is a traditional breakfast in West Africa (though it also works as a healthy dessert). This dish calls for black millet, which can be found at African grocery stores. As it absorbs water, it plumps up. If you can't find black millet, regular millet can be used as a substitute. The traditional version of this pudding doesn't include granola and blueberries, but they were added for Eat Offbeat's customers, so they are included here as optional.

1 cup black millet
(or regular millet)

4 cups sour cream

½ cup whole milk

½ cup sugar

Granola, for serving (optional)

Blueberries, for serving (optional)

Ground cinnamon, for garnish
(optional)

1 Pour 2 cups of water into a large saucepan, place over high heat, and bring to a boil. Stir in the millet, then lower the heat to a simmer. Simmer, covered, until the water is absorbed and the millet is tender, about 15 minutes. Remove from the heat and let cool.

2 Whisk the sour cream, milk, and sugar together in a large mixing bowl. When they are fully combined, stir in the millet (reserving a few spoonfuls of the millet for garnish, if desired).

3 Serve the degué in small bowls, topping with granola, blueberries, a spoonful of the reserved millet, and a dusting of cinnamon, if desired.

─BOFLOT─

Fried dough puff puffs rolled in cinnamon-sugar dust

─ MAKES 18 PUFF PUFFS ─

Most people don't associate African street food with doughnuts, but boflot are essentially doughnut bites. Minata's version is coated in cinnamon sugar.

2 cups lukewarm water (105°F to 110°F)

1 tablespoon granulated sugar

2¼ teaspoons (1 envelope) active dry yeast

1½ teaspoons kosher salt

2 cups confectioners' sugar

2 tablespoons ground cinnamon

4 cups unbleached all-purpose flour

Vegetable oil, for deep-frying

1 Whisk together the water, granulated sugar, and yeast in a large mixing bowl. Once everything is incorporated, let it sit until foamy, about 5 minutes.

2 Once the water is foamy, whisk in the salt and flour. Cover the bowl with plastic wrap and let the dough rest in a warm place until it has doubled, at least 1 hour.

3 Meanwhile, whisk the confectioners' sugar and cinnamon together in a medium mixing bowl. Set aside.

4 Pour the oil into a large heavy-bottomed stockpot or Dutch oven to a depth of at least 2 inches and clip a candy thermometer to the side, making sure it doesn't touch the bottom. Heat the oil to 375°F over high heat, then lower the heat to medium to maintain the temperature during frying.

5 Carefully scoop the dough into small tablespoon-size balls and place them in the oil with a slotted spoon. Working in batches and being careful not to crowd the pot, deep-fry the dough until golden brown, 9 to 10 minutes. Remove the boflot with a mesh strainer and toss in the cinnamon-sugar mix. When thoroughly coated, place on a serving plate. Repeat with the remaining dough and cinnamon sugar. Serve immediately.

CHEF MINATA

GUINEA

MINATA KABA'S LIFE BACK IN KANKAN, GUINEA, CENTERED AROUND COOKING and cleaning. As the oldest of six children, she shouldered the responsibility of cooking daily meals for her family, as well as hosting any extended family who lived nearby. This often meant planning for upwards of twenty people at least twice a day.

Thankfully, Minata was taught how to handle the role of hostess by her mother, Jinab, who herself had to host about a dozen people a few times a day. (And Minata still hears her mother's voice in her head when preparing food.) Jinab would have to wake up in the wee hours of the morning to prepare breakfast. Even though Kankan is Guinea's third-largest city, many people live there without electricity, meaning almost all cooking is done over an open fire. After the morning meal was done and cleaned up, it was time to go to the market. Minata remembers how her mother taught her which vendors sold the best produce and how to pick the ripest pieces. Then it was time for lunch, finishing up any hand washing for the day, and getting ready for dinner. Later on, Jinab would send Minata to the market alone, fully trusting that the young girl would know exactly what to buy.

As an adult, Minata found time most afternoons for her side hustle of importing and selling clothing and other goods from neighboring countries. She often took the bus to Côte d'Ivoire and Mali to buy inventory and turn a profit back in Kankan. Here in the United States, she's pursuing something similar, selling clothes and fabrics imported directly from West Africa.

Prior to working at Eat Offbeat, Minata was an assistant gardener at another IRC project, the New Roots Community Farm. Located on a half-acre plot in the Bronx, New Roots includes small raised-bed plots, hoop houses, and honeybee hives. The IRC uses the site to offer new refugees on-the-job training, English classes, and the opportunity to grow their own food. It was there that Minata first encountered fellow Eat Offbeat chefs Larissa and Rose, two chefs she's close to in the kitchen. And it's that sense of familiarity, of being a part of a larger community, that's helped Minata flourish in the Eat Offbeat kitchen.

ROLLED BAKLAVA

Sweet phyllo pastry stuffed
with cardamom-spiced pistachios

◁ MAKES 15 SERVINGS ▷

Baklava is the sweet treat of choice in Iraq. But since it's so ubiquitous—and time-consuming to create—people generally do not make baklava from scratch at home. You simply pick it up from one of the many shops in your town. Baklava also comes in a wide variety of regional styles, from the honey-soaked rolled baklava in Greece to the rose water–soaked diamond baklava of Iran, each a flaky phyllo-layered dish that's filled with nuts.

---

1 pound shelled pistachio nuts

1 can (10 ounces) sweetened condensed milk

1 roll (8 ounces) phyllo dough, defrosted (Athens brand or similar)

1 cup (2 sticks) unsalted butter, melted

½ cup sugar

5 green cardamom pods

---

1 Preheat the oven to 350°F and line a rimmed sheet pan with parchment paper. Soak clean cotton dishcloths or paper towels with water and wring out the excess moisture.

2 Pulse the pistachio nuts in a food processor until the pieces are uniform and roughly the size of peppercorns, about 25 pulses. Reserve 2 tablespoons of ground pistachios for garnish, if desired. Pour the remaining pistachios into a medium mixing bowl and stir in the condensed milk.

3 On a clean work surface, carefully unfold the roll of phyllo dough, peel off one sheet, and set the rest aside, covered with the damp cloths or paper towels to keep the dough from drying out.

4 Brush the phyllo sheet with the butter. Unfold another phyllo sheet on top and brush it with butter. Repeat with two more phyllo sheets. Once you have a stack of four buttered sheets, spoon a line of the pistachio mixture along the longer side of the phyllo. Carefully roll the stack of phyllo, covering the filling, jelly roll– or cigar-style, using gentle pressure to hold its shape, all the way to the top of the dough.

5   Slice the roll into 1½ to 2-inch pieces. Place the pieces on the prepared sheet pan and bake until golden, about 20 minutes.

6   While the baklava is baking, place the sugar, ½ cup of water, and the cardamom pods in a small saucepan over medium-high heat, stirring frequently with a spatula to dissolve the sugar. When the mixture comes to a boil, about 3 minutes, remove the pan from the heat and set aside.

7   When the baklava is done, take it out of the oven and generously spoon the cardamom syrup over the pieces. Sprinkle with the reserved ground pistachios, if desired. Let cool completely on a wire rack before serving.

DREAMY IRAQI DESSERT

To watch Dhuha making her baklava in the Eat Offbeat kitchen is like watching an origami master—every roll and slice of the dough is perfectly symmetrical, and the flaky, soft dough is an artwork dotted with fragrant chopped pistachios. There are many different ways to slice and roll baklava, but at home Dhuha makes it in a tray and then cuts it into the shape she wants.

Another of her favorite desserts, *knafeh*, is similar to baklava—it's a phyllo and pistachio creation made of golden pastry noodles (called "hair") over a base of salty cheese and sticky syrup scented with rose and orange blossom water, baked until the cheese oozes and the top is crispy. Dhuha says that some recipes include a dye that gives the dish a special color. It's actually an herb that's used to make the dessert orange—similar to saffron—and she remembers making it in Iraq all the time.

─ CAKE BAKLAVA ─

*A dry, nutty cake spiced with
cardamom and saffron*

◅ MAKES ONE 9-INCH ROUND CAKE ▻

Flaky baklava, with its layers of sweetness and nuts, is delicious when made into a cake. It keeps all the same flavors with walnuts, almonds, and pistachios being added to the batter. If you want additional sweetness for the final cake, poke holes in the top and brush the cake with honey, or top with a honey-based frosting. The sweetness will round out the cake's nuttiness.

1 cup (2 sticks) butter, softened, plus more for greasing the pan

¾ cup (4 ounces) shelled pistachios, plus 1 tablespoon chopped pistachios for garnish

1 cup (4 ounces) shelled walnuts

⅔ cup (4 ounces) whole raw almonds

1 cup all-purpose flour

1 teaspoon baking powder

2 teaspoons ground cardamom

1 cup sugar

4 large eggs

3 tablespoons saffron water (see Note)

Chopped pistachios, for garnish

1 Preheat the oven to 350°F. Line a 9-inch round cake pan with parchment paper and grease lightly with butter.

2 Grind each type of nut separately in a food processor, setting each aside.

3 Place the flour, baking powder, and cardamom in a small mixing bowl. Whisk to fully combine. Set aside.

4 Place the butter in the bowl of a stand mixer. With the paddle attachment, beat the butter on low speed until it begins to break up, about 30 seconds. Increase the speed to medium and beat for 1 minute. Stop the mixer to scrape down the sides of the bowl. Increase the mixer speed to medium and slowly add the sugar. Continue beating until the butter and sugar are creamed, about 5 minutes.

RECIPE CONTINUES

5   Reduce the mixer speed to medium-low and add the eggs one at a time, beating for 30 seconds after each one to incorporate and scraping down the sides of the bowl as needed. Once all the eggs have been added, increase the speed to medium and beat until fully incorporated, about 2 minutes.

6   Reduce the mixer speed to low and slowly add the flour mixture in three parts, beating for 30 seconds after each addition. Increase the speed to medium and beat until the batter is light and fluffy, about 3 minutes.

7   Reduce the mixer speed to medium-low and slowly add the ground nuts and the saffron water to the batter. Beat until the nuts are fully incorporated, about 5 minutes. Scrape down the sides of the bowl, as needed.

8   Using a rubber spatula, fill the prepared cake pan with the batter, leveling the top to smooth it. Bake until the top is golden and a cake tester inserted into the center comes out clean, 30 to 35 minutes. Sprinkle the chopped pistachios over the top in the last 5 minutes of baking. Let cool completely on a wire rack before serving.

NOTE   According to Nasrin, the foolproof way to get saffron into this cake is to grind 4 threads of it in a spice grinder with 1 teaspoon of sugar and then place that mixture in a bowl with 4 ice cubes. When the ice melts, the saffron will have infused the water, which can be added to the cake batter.

CONVERSION TABLES

Please note that all conversions are approximate but close enough to be useful when converting from one system to another.

OVEN TEMPERATURES

FAHRENHEIT	GAS MARK	CELSIUS
250	½	120
275	1	140
300	2	150
325	3	160
350	4	180
375	5	190
400	6	200
425	7	220
450	8	230
475	9	240
500	10	260

NOTE: Reduce the temperature by 20°C (68°F) for fan-assisted ovens.

APPROXIMATE EQUIVALENTS

1 stick butter = 8 tbs = 4 oz = ½ cup = 115 g

1 cup all-purpose presifted flour = 4.7 oz

1 cup granulated sugar = 8 oz = 220 g

1 cup (firmly packed) brown sugar = 6 oz = 220 g to 230 g

1 cup confectioners' sugar = 4½ oz = 115 g

1 cup honey or syrup = 12 oz

1 cup grated cheese = 4 oz

1 cup dried beans = 6 oz

1 large egg = about 2 oz or about 3 tbs

1 egg yolk = about 1 tbs

1 egg white = about 2 tbs

LIQUID CONVERSIONS

U.S.	IMPERIAL	METRIC
2 tbs	1 fl oz	30 ml
3 tbs	1½ fl oz	45 ml
¼ cup	2 fl oz	60 ml
⅓ cup	2½ fl oz	75 ml
⅓ cup + 1 tbs	3 fl oz	90 ml
⅓ cup + 2 tbs	3½ fl oz	100 ml
½ cup	4 fl oz	125 ml
⅔ cup	5 fl oz	150 ml
¾ cup	6 fl oz	175 ml
¾ cup + 2 tbs	7 fl oz	200 ml
1 cup	8 fl oz	250 ml
1 cup + 2 tbs	9 fl oz	275 ml
1¼ cups	10 fl oz	300 ml
1⅓ cups	11 fl oz	325 ml
1½ cups	12 fl oz	350 ml
1⅔ cups	13 fl oz	375 ml
1¾ cups	14 fl oz	400 ml
1¾ cups + 2 tbs	15 fl oz	450 ml
2 cups (1 pint)	16 fl oz	500 ml
2½ cups	20 fl oz (1 pint)	600 ml
3¾ cups	1½ pints	900 ml
4 cups	1¾ pints	1 liter

WEIGHT CONVERSIONS

U.S./U.K.	METRIC	U.S./U.K.	METRIC
½ oz	15 g	7 oz	200 g
1 oz	30 g	8 oz	250 g
1½ oz	45 g	9 oz	275 g
2 oz	60 g	10 oz	300 g
2½ oz	75 g	11 oz	325 g
3 oz	90 g	12 oz	350 g
3½ oz	100 g	13 oz	375 g
4 oz	125 g	14 oz	400 g
5 oz	150 g	15 oz	450 g
6 oz	175 g	1 lb	500 g

CONTRIBUTORS

CHEF JUAN SUAREZ DE LEZO says that food was an important part of his childhood in Córdoba, Spain. His mother and grandmother were chefs who worked in restaurants and wrote a prize-winning book together. Juan got his bearings in the kitchen watching and working with them, waking up early on his summer vacations to bake with his grandmother—a source of happy memories as well as professional-level training. But it wasn't until he was in his late twenties that Juan would decide to become a chef.

After a stint working as a journalist, Juan's parents urged him to study cooking. He attended Le Cordon Bleu in Paris, and his skill and deep, life-long love of cooking paid off. He worked at restaurants boasting thirteen Michelin stars among them, including El Bulli and Arzak in Spain, Maido in Peru, and Per Se in New York City.

Juan came to Eat Offbeat through connections at Columbia Business School. He joined the kitchen in 2015 as one of the first team members, curating and perfecting the chefs' dishes. He continues as Eat Offbeat's culinary advisor and chief culinary officer.

SIOBHAN WALLACE has written for *Wine Enthusiast, Food52, Extra Crispy, Edible Queens, Food & Wine, Serious Eats,* and *Citysearch.* Prior to *The Kitchen without Borders,* she coauthored *New York à la Cart: Recipes and Stories from the Big Apple's Best Food Trucks* (Running Press, 2013) with Alexandra Penfold. She lives in Brooklyn, New York, with her cat, Lady.

PENNY DE LOS SANTOS is an award-winning internationally published photographer, senior contributing photographer to *Saveur Magazine,* and a regular contributing photographer for *National Geographic.* She has received numerous grants, fellowships, and awards for her photography, and her work has been featured in magazines including *Martha Stewart Living, Bon Appétit, Time, Newsweek, Sports Illustrated, Latina, Texas Monthly,* and *U.S. News & World Report.* Penny has been a featured speaker at many universities and industry conferences throughout the country, and her TEDx Talk on photography has been viewed more than 18,000 times. She lives in New York City with her dog, Nigella.

ACKNOWLEDGMENTS

THIS COOKBOOK WOULD NOT HAVE GOTTEN INTO YOUR HANDS IF IT weren't for all the incredible people who have made our Eat Offbeat journey possible.

We want to start by acknowledging all the chefs who poured their love, their passion, and their cherished memories into these pages. Thank you for being the vibrant power that moves our kitchen every day. Scaling your home cooking to such levels is no easy feat, but you make it seem like a piece of cake. Thank you to Chef Juan who believed in the team's talent since day one and has helped it bloom ever since. To the incredible delivery team, who consistently and wholeheartedly supports our chefs every single day. To Courtney, Jovier, Satakshi, Adriana, Rosemary, Sarujen, Alexandra, Colin, Celine, Jahangir, Altaf, who have worn different hats at Eat Offbeat and who each played a role in shaping our chefs' journeys and recipes. To our friends and partners at the IRC's New York office— Avigail, Kathleen, Pema, and Maria—who introduced us to all the amazing people who make up the Eat Offbeat family today.

Thank you to everyone at the Tamer Center for Social Enterprise that believed in us and supported us before we even had a kitchen to call home. To the Columbia Startup Lab for being our home for a few years. To Sarah, Jolyne, and all our friends and advisors, who continue to push us forward. And to the WeWork Creator Awards team for taking our growth to the next level.

Running a Kickstarter campaign for this cookbook was a whole new ball game for us. Nadi, you were the rockstar we needed to fulfill this dream—thank you for helping us exceed our expectations. Hanane, thank you for your beautiful designs and your magical touch, and Signe, thank you for all your advice. Lena, your genuine filmmaking talent, and Izzy, your incredible music, were key to the campaign's success. Sarita and Raj, we can't thank you enough for opening up your home to us to shoot the video.

Thank you, Sandra, for your generous contribution to the Kickstarter campaign, as well as to Chef Philippe, Jeremie, Pao, Susie, Yvette, Mirey, Zachary, Jeanne, Jacqueline, and Carine for being top contributors. To the 1,745 other backers: We are still overwhelmed by your support. YOU made this happen and for that we will forever be grateful.

We have now learned how incredibly arduous producing a cookbook can be. We would never have made it without the patient and gracious support of the team at Workman.

To Liz Davis Saunders—thank you for the endless trips to our kitchen, long phone calls, late-night texts, for your patience with our delays, and for your determination to keep each recipe and each story as genuine as can be. To Siobhan Wallace—for graciously interviewing all the chefs and transcending all language barriers, and for meticulously testing and re-testing every single one of our recipes. To the photo shoot team: Penny De Los Santos, Nora Singley, Alyssa Kondracki, Sara Abalan, Jay Kim, and Stephanie Munguia—you gave our dishes and our team the treatment of movie stars. To Kylie Foxx McDonald, Rae Ann Spitzenberger, Anne Kerman, Hillary Leary, Suzie Bolotin, Jenny Mandel, Rebecca Carlisle, Moira Kerrigan, and Chloe Puton for all your work and support before, during, and after publication. And to Leanne Brown and Robert Gehorsham who connected the dots and introduced us to this incredible team.

Special thoughts to our Teta Jano, whose famous hummus recipe and whose tenacity inspired us and still inspires us every day, and to Tante Margo and all our aunts whose exceptional home cooking we long for.

And finally, to Hyam, Abdo, and Hala, who knew something was cooking before we even lit the fire. To Natasha for keeping an eye on us. And to Karim, first believer in this cookbook and biggest supporter through the highs and the lows.

Much love,
Manal and Wissam

RECIPES BY CHEF

INDEX

(Page references in *italics* refer to illustrations.)

Cauliflower, Manchurian,
    115–17, *116*
Central African Republic
    (Chef Larissa), 59–60, *61*
    red pepper soup, *62*, 63
Central African Republic
    (Chef Rose), *94*, 95–96
Cachapas, *18*, 19
Chari bari, 138–40, *139*
Chari curry, 157
Char magaz, xvii, *122*, 123
Cheddar cheese, in fatayer,
    13–14, *15*
Cheese:
    cachapas, *18*, 19
    cheddar, in fatayer, 13–14, *15*
    feta, in salad shirazi, 45
    Gorgonzola, in Egyptian
        moussaka, *166*, 167–68
    mozzarella, in ma'areena
        soup, 64, *65*
    mozzarella, in Nepali pizza,
        126, 127–28
    see also Paneer cheese
Chestnuts, in ouzé, 92–93
Chicken:
    Algerian couscous, 68–69
    chari bari, 138–40, *139*
    chari curry, 157
    chu la, 144–45
    cilantro, 169
    fatayer, 13–14, *15*
    fesenjan, 136–37
    karahi, 134, *135*
    Minata's okra, 98–99, *99*
    poulet yassa, 172
    riz gras, 82–83, *83*
    shawarma, 170
Chickpea(s):
    Algerian couscous, 68–69
    flour, in Manchurian
        cauliflower, 115–17, *116*

hummus, *22*, 23
musabbaha, 39
rooz, 87–89, *88*
Chiles:
    bird's-eye (also known as
        Thai chile and piri piri), xvii
    Kashmiri, xviii
Chocolate, in sumac brownie,
    186, 187
Chu la, 144–45
Cider vinaigrette, 46
Cilantro:
    chicken, 169
    kuku sabzi, 20, *21*
    lemon dressing, 55
Coconut cabbage, 104, *105*
Coconut milk:
    bonji carrot curry, 106
    Shanthi's dhal, 102
Conversion tables, 199
Corn, in cachapas, *18*, 19
Couscous:
    Algerian, 68–69
    origin of word, 69
    Shanthi's, 73
Croquettes (kibbeh), 9
    beef, 7–8
    potato, *10*, 11–12
Cucumber:
    edamame salad, 46, *47*
    fattoush, 52, *53*
    salad shirazi, 45
    sumac salad, 44
Curry:
    bhindi (okra and potato), 129
    bonji carrot, 106
    chari (chicken thighs), 157
    chu la (ground chicken),
        144–45
    colonialism and, 145
    kanawa (squid), 141–43, *142*
    katarica (eggplant), 124–25, *125*

paneer, thickened with spices
    and melon seeds, 122–23
paneer and peas, 118–20, *119*
Curry leaves, xvii
    dosas, 103
    kowa varrai, 104, *105*
    Shanthi's couscous, 73
    Shanthi's dhal, 102
    see also Curry

D

Date truffles, 185
Degué, 188, *189*
De Lezo, Juan Suarez, 200
Desserts, 176–77, 185–98
    boflot, 190
    cake baklava, 196–98, *197*
    date truffles, 185
    degué, 188, *189*
    knafeh, 195
    rolled baklava, 194–95
    sumac brownie, *186*, 187
Dhal:
    Shanthi's (split lentil), 102
    toor (yellow lentil), 110
    urad (spicy black lentil), 111
Digestive biscuits, in sumac
    brownie, *186*, 187
Dill, in kuku sabzi, 20, *21*
Dipping sauce, savory, 3
Dips, 22–40
    baba ghannoush, 33
    borani esfenaj, 36, *37*
    hummus, *22*, 23
    kashk bademjan, 30–32, *31*
    mirza ghasemi, 28–29
    musabbaha, 39
Dolmas, Mitslal's, 130–31, *131*
Doogh:
    Bashir's, 182, *183*
    Nasrin's, 184
Dosas, 103

The International Rescue Committee responds to the world's worst humanitarian crises, helping to restore health, safety, education, economic wellbeing, and power to people devastated by conflict and disaster. Founded in 1933 at the call of Albert Einstein, the IRC is at work in over 40 countries and 26 offices across the U.S. helping people to survive, reclaim control of their future, and strengthen their communities. Learn more at **www.rescue.org/cookbook**